THE KITCHEN

AND

DINING ROOM

TRADITIONAL
WOODWORKING

THE KITCHEN

AND

DINING ROOM

Step-by-step projects
for the woodworker

Watson-Guptill Publications/New York

First published in the United States by
Watson-Guptill Publications
a division of BPI Communications, Inc.
1515 Broadway, New York, N. Y. 10036

Originally published by Collins & Brown Ltd
London House, Great Eastern Wharf
Parkgate Road, London SW11 4NQ

ISBN 0-8230-5403-9

Library of Congress Catalog Card Number: 98-86429

A NOTE ON SAFETY

For the purposes of visual clarity in step-by-step photographs, safety guards
on power tools have at times been removed. Always refer to the manufacturer's
safety instructions when working with any power or machine tool.

Series Editor: Liz Dean
Project Editor: Ian Kearey
Editorial Assistant: Lisa Balkwill
Designer: Alison Verity
Original Design: Suzanne Metcalfe-Megginson
Illustrator: Keith Field

Editorial Director: Sarah Hoggett
Art Director: Roger Bristow

Printed in China

First printing, 1998

1 2 3 4 5 6 7 8 9 / 06 05 04 03 02 01 00 99 98

CONTENTS

Introduction 6

THE PROJECTS

FINISHING

INTRODUCTION

THE PROFESSIONAL AND amateur furniture makers who designed and created these projects were selected for their classic and timeless designs, high-quality craftsmanship, innovative techniques and, not least, the ability to explain precisely how their pieces can be made. These inspiring projects reflect a range of woodworking skills, and with their clear and detailed instructions, step-by-step photographs and color exploded diagrams, they are well within the grasp of all enthusiastic woodworkers.

Of all the rooms in the house, by their very nature the kitchen and dining room offer perhaps the widest range of furniture styles that can be used – the functional simplicity and elegance of Shaker-based designs, such as the Shaker Drawers (p. 64) and Kitchen Wall Unit (p. 46); the traditional, gentle country shapes of the Country Kitchen Table (p. 40) and Wheelback Kitchen Chair (p. 30), or the clean lines of more modern designs, such as the Wine Rack (p. 70) and Plate Drying Rack (p. 10).

In the same way, there is a great range of materials to choose from: hardwoods and softwoods, of course, but also blockboard and chipboard for worktop surfaces and matching units, such as the Limed Cupboard (p. 24), and much of the construction of the Oak Breakfront (p. 52).

Tools and Materials

A good basic set of hand tools, well sharpened and maintained, is essential. This should include a workbench, marking devices – try squares, steel rules, marking knife, mortise gauge and pencil – a selection of screwdrivers, chisels, planes, hammer, mallet, drill, sharpening equipment, and basic saws, such as a tenon saw, coping saw, ripsaw, and dovetail saw. A selection of grades of sandpaper, from fine to coarse, is also essential for final preparation of the wood before finishing the project.

These days most workshops, however small, have a selection of power tools, such as a drill, jigsaw, router, and sander, and these items can be invaluable when tackling some of the jobs involved. If you do have access to machine tools, this will also help you with your project work. However, a number of the projects have been designed to be made by hand tools in the first instance, so power tools are not always essential.

When you are choosing timber, bear in mind that wooden items in the kitchen may be regularly subjected to considerable wear and tear, particularly steam and splashes of food and liquids. Therefore, consider the function of your chosen project when purchasing timber. Each of the twelve projects presented in this book incorporates a full cutting list which specifies required measurements for timber and other materials, all of which can be purchased at your local lumber yard. This is certainly preferable to buying timber from a home improvement store, because the selection will be larger and the wood will be cut to meet your specifications.

Finishing

It is always a good idea to consider the finish for a project before starting. In this book, each project includes advice on the finish that was used by the designer, and alternatives are also shown. One finish for kitchen fittings and furniture that has revived in popularity over recent years is liming; in the past, this was a long and somewhat hazardous process, but modern technological advances have made it possible to create attractive plain and colored limed finishes, which are described in detail with step-by-step photographs in the Finishing section (pp. 74–77). Similarly, the subtle glow of French

LEFT: *This Cherry Dining Table (p. 14) is based on a classic design.*

RIGHT: *The Kitchen Wall Unit (p. 46) is a relatively simple project that looks good in the kitchen or dining room.*

polish is the perfect accompaniment to an elegant dining table or sideboard, but achieving this finish has long been shrouded in mystery and difficulty. However, there is no reason why a simplified, brushed-on French polish should not be used to create the desired finish, and this technique is also included. As with the projects themselves, you can adapt the finishes to suit your overall room decor.

We hope that you enjoy making the projects in this book, and that the designs and finishing techniques shown here may inspire you to create your own furniture and fittings throughout the house.

PLATE DRYING RACK

*This traditional rack is made using modern techniques, and it should, ideally, be placed
above the kitchen drain board to catch dripping water. The depth needs
to be at least 11 in (280 mm), to hold the average-sized dinner plate,
but you can adjust the other measurements as required.*

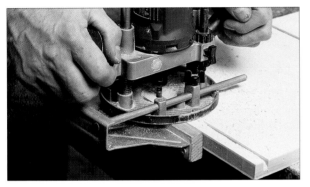

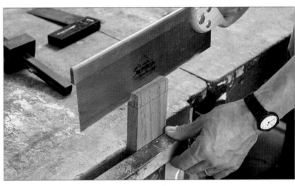

1 First mark out the blockboard for the carcass. Using
a circular saw fitted with a fine cross-cut blade, cut out
the sides, top and shelf. Apply beech edge-banding with an
iron; trim the excess with medium-grade sandpaper.
To make the stopped dovetail housing joint, cut $\frac{3}{8}$-in
(10-mm) deep stopped grooves in the side pieces using a
power router and $\frac{1}{4}$–$\frac{5}{8}$ in (6–16 mm) cutter.

2 Fit a rabbeting bit to the router and set the depth stop
to leave a tongue the same thickness as the groove in
the side pieces. Cut a rabbet on each end of the top and
shelf. Cut off enough of the tongue to negotiate the stop
on the groove, then dry-assemble the carcass to test-fit the
joints. Mock-up a section to estimate the gaps between the
centers of the dowels – usually $1\frac{1}{8}$ in (30 mm).

3 Mark cross-rails and center-punch holes for drilling,
using an electric drill fitted to a stand. Cut the dowel
to equal lengths, sand blemishes with medium-grade
sandpaper, then sand cross-rails. Glue horizontal-rack
dowels with waterproof PVA. When set, glue vertical-rack
dowels. Before leaving the rack to set, use a try square to
check the angle between the dowels and cross-rail is 90°.

4 Draw the profile of half a pelmet onto paper and
trace the profile onto a piece of hardboard or plywood.
Next, cut out the shape with a jigsaw to make a template.
Lay the template on the 3 x 1 in (75 x 25 mm) planed
softwood, draw around it, then flip template and repeat
(see inset). Smooth the edges with sandpaper. Cut out with
a jigsaw and finish the edge with sandpaper and files.

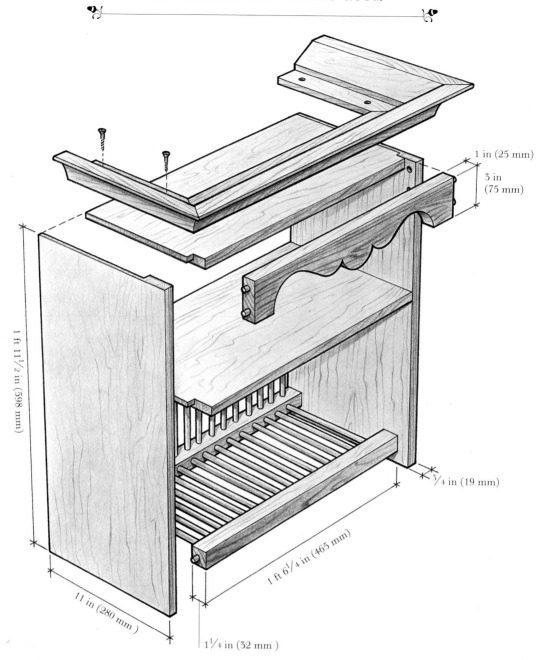

1 in (25 mm)

3 in (75 mm)

1 ft 11½ in (598 mm)

³⁄₄ in (19 mm)

1 ft 6¼ in (465 mm)

11 in (280 mm)

1¼ in (32 mm)

Sealing the Cabinet

There are several advantages to sealing the cabinet before final assembly. Sealing makes it easier to handle the individual pieces, and you will achieve a better surface finish when sandpapering and varnishing.

In addition, the excess adhesive that oozes out of the joints when you are gluing together the cabinet can be wiped off easily with a damp cloth, without the danger of staining the timber.

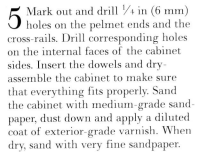

5 Mark out and drill ¼ in (6 mm) holes on the pelmet ends and the cross-rails. Drill corresponding holes on the internal faces of the cabinet sides. Insert the dowels and dry-assemble the cabinet to make sure that everything fits properly. Sand the cabinet with medium-grade sandpaper, dust down and apply a diluted coat of exterior-grade varnish. When dry, sand with very fine sandpaper.

6 Apply waterproof adhesive to the joints. Assemble cabinet and secure it with bar clamps, packing scrap wood into the clamp jaws. Wipe off excess adhesive and check that the corners are at 90°. Leave to set, then mark out the cornice and cut it at 45° with a cross-cut saw in a miter block. Apply adhesive to the joints, hold together with masking tape and leave to set overnight.

7 Sand and varnish the cornice as described in Step 5. Drill ⁵⁄₁₆ in (5 mm) countersunk clearance holes in the cornice base and screw it to the top of the cabinet with No. 8 1¼ in (32 mm) plated or brass screws. Finish off by applying a final coat of varnish to the cabinet and fix it to the wall with brass hanging plates.

LIST OF MATERIALS (*measurements indicate cut size*)

ITEM	SECTION	LENGTH
Birch-faced blockboard for sides, 2, top, 1, and shelf, 1	11 x ¾ in (280 x 11 mm)	7ft 1 in (2166 mm)
Iron-on beech edge banding	¾ in (19 mm)	5ft 6 in (1675 mm)
Softwood for pelmet, 1, and cornice, 1	3 x 1 in (75 x 25 mm)	5 ft 6¼ in (1684 mm)
Softwood for cross-rails, 2	1¼ x 1¼ in (32 x 32 mm)	3ft ½ in (970 mm)
Ramin dowels, 30	⁵⁄₁₆ in (8 mm) diameter	25 ft 4 in (7700 mm)
No. 8 plated screws		1¼ in (32 mm)
Exterior varnish, brass hanging plates		

CHERRY DINING TABLE

*The clean lines and sturdy construction
of this Shaker-inspired dining table make
it an elegant centerpiece for any kitchen or dining
room. It is built using butt, mortise-and-tenon,
dovetail and dowel joints, and can be made
from a variety of woods.*

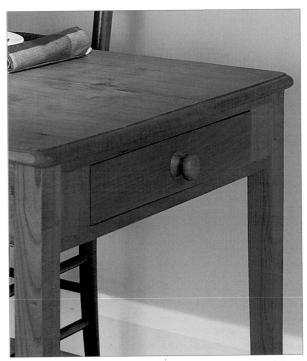

The top is made from four boards joined by biscuits.

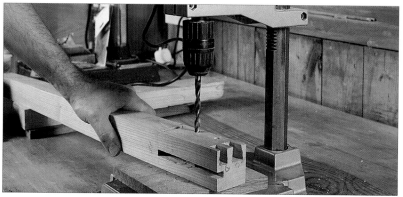

1 Cut the boards for the top to 5 ft (1530 mm) length. Plane the meeting edges square with a jack plane, and cut three or four slots for biscuits along them, using a biscuit joiner. Glue and insert biscuits, apply glue along the meeting edges and clamp the top together, alternating bar clamps on the top and underside. When dry, clamp the assembled top to the bench and sand it down.

2 Cut the legs, then place in two pairs – one for the side and end rails, and two for the side and drawer rails. Use a mortise gauge to mark out the twin mortises for the side and end rails on the inner faces of the "1" pair, and the side rails on the "2" pair; on the other faces of the "2" pair, mark out mortises for stub tenons for the lower drawer rail, and dovetails for the top drawer rail. Taper the inside faces of all four legs to $1\frac{1}{2}$ in (38 mm) square, using a circular saw, then clean up with a jack plane and cabinet scraper. Drill out the waste for the mortises using a $\frac{1}{4}$ in (6 mm) drill bit, and chop the rest out using $\frac{1}{4}$ and 1 in (6 and 25 mm) bevel-edged chisels. Cut out the dovetails in the "2" pair using a dovetail saw.

3 Mark and cut the end rail to 2 ft $2\frac{3}{4}$ in (679 mm) and the side rails to 4 ft $7\frac{3}{4}$ in (1416 mm). Use a mortise gauge to mark the ends for the edges and the twin haunched stub tenons. Cut the tenons with a tenon saw, and use a miter saw to cut off the waste on the shoulder lines. Cut drawer rails to 2 ft $2\frac{1}{2}$ in (673 mm), then cut the dovetails to match the legs in the top rail, and the stub tenons in the bottom rail. Drill guide holes for evenly spaced brass stretcher plates in the inside top edges of the end and side rails, for joining to the top – three in each side rail and two in the end rail (see inset).

4 Mark and cut the center rail to 2 ft $4\frac{3}{8}$ in (721 mm), then mark out the dovetails for attaching to the side rails with a dovetail template or square. Cut the dovetails with a tenon saw, then use a miter saw to cut the waste to the shoulder line. Hold the center rail to the side rails, and mark and cut the matching dovetails in the side rails. Fit the center and side rails, and adjust as required. Mark and cut the upright blanks to $3\frac{1}{2}$ in (90 mm) length, and drill $\frac{5}{16}$ in (8 mm) dowel holes in the end edges and the inside faces of the "2" pair of legs.

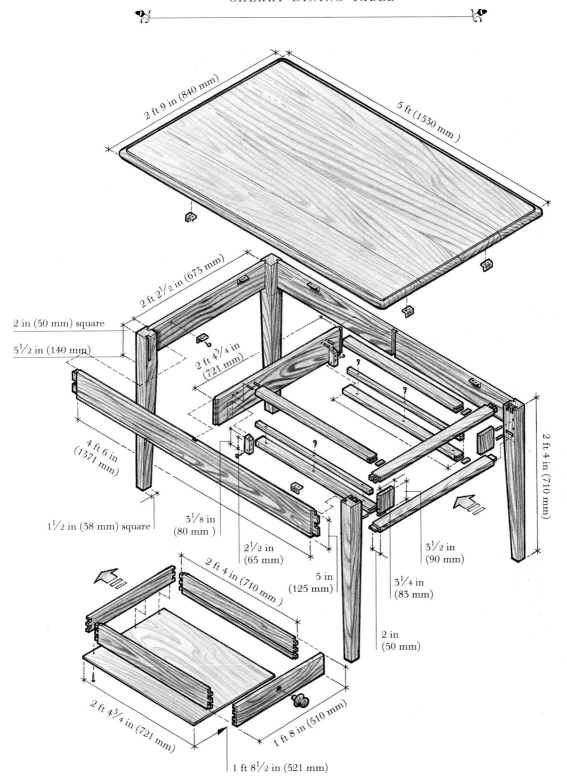

2 ft 9 in (840 mm)

5 ft (1530 mm)

2 ft 2½ in (673 mm)

2 in (50 mm) square

5½ in (140 mm)

2 ft 4¾ in
(721 mm)

2 ft 4 in
(710 mm)

4 ft 6 in
(1371 mm)

1½ in (38 mm) square

3⅛ in
(80 mm)

2½ in
(65 mm)

5 in
(125 mm)

3½ in
(90 mm)

3¼ in
(83 mm)

2 in
(50 mm)

2 ft 4 in (710 mm)

2 ft 4¾ in (721 mm)

1 ft 8 in (510 mm)

1 ft 8½ in (521 mm)

17

5 Dry-assemble legs, rails, and blanks, holding the frame with bar clamps, and checking for square. Cut drawer runners, kickers and guides to 2 ft 2¼ in (665 mm). Cut ¼ x ¼ in (6 x 6 mm) grooves ¾ in (19 mm) into the outside end of the drawer runners and the matching inside top edge of the bottom drawer rail, and cut ¾-in (19-mm) long plywood tongues to fit the grooves. Cut similar grooves and tongues for the outside end of the drawer kickers and the matching inside bottom edge of the top drawer rail. Drill ⁵⁄₁₆ in (8 mm) dowel holes in the other end of the drawer kickers and in the center rail. Cut the drawer runner blocks to 3⅛ in (80 mm), and glue and screw them to the center rail.

6 Take the frame assembly apart and cut a ⅛ in (4 mm) bead along the bottom outside edge of the end and side rails, using a router. Cut the drawer front and back to 1 ft 8 in (510 mm), the drawer sides to 2 ft 4 in (710 mm), and the drawer bottom to 2 ft 4⅜ in (721 mm). Cut a ¼ in (6 mm) groove above the bottom edge of the front and sides, to fit the bottom. Mark and cut through-dovetails on the back and matching sides, and hidden dovetails on the front and matching sides. Apply glue to the dovetail joints and clamp the drawer frame, checking for square. When dry, slide the bottom into the groove and fix with small screws into the bottom edge of the back. Drill a pilot hole in the drawer front and fit the knob.

7 Glue and clamp the end rail and "2" pair of legs and then the drawer rails, upright blanks and "1" pair of legs. When dry, glue and clamp the side and center rails to the end-frame assemblies. Screw the drawer runner blocks on the center rail to the drawer runners, and glue in the tongues to the other end of the runners and the bottom drawer rail. Screw the drawer guides to the top surfaces and sides of the runners. Glue in the tongues to the drawer kickers and top drawer rail, and dowel the other end of the kickers to the center rail.

8 Screw the stretcher plates to the side and end rails and the upright blanks, then place the top in position on the frame and mark and drill pilot holes in the underside of the top. Screw the top to the stretcher plates. Plane the ends of the top square, then use a router to round the corners and cut a decorative molding on the edges. Sand the top with progressively finer grades of sandpaper, clean up the whole table and drawer, and finish.

LIST OF MATERIALS *(measurements indicate cut size)*

ITEM	SECTION	LENGTH
Hardwood/softwood for top, 1	2 ft 9 in x $\frac{7}{8}$ in (840 x 21 mm)	5 ft (1530 mm)
Hardwood/softwood for legs, 4	2 x 2 in (50 x 50 mm)	9 ft 4 in (2840 mm)
Hardwood/softwood for end rail, 1, side rails, 2, and center rail, 1	5 x $\frac{3}{4}$ in (125 x 19 mm)	13 ft 10 $\frac{5}{8}$ in (4232 mm)
Hardwood/softwood for drawer rails, 2	2 x $\frac{3}{4}$ in (50 x 19 mm)	4 ft 5 in (1345 mm)
Hardwood/softwood for upright blanks, 2	$3\frac{1}{4}$ x $\frac{3}{4}$ in (83 x 19 mm)	7 in (178 mm)
Hardwood/softwood for drawer runners, 2, and drawer kickers, 2	$1\frac{3}{4}$ x $\frac{3}{4}$ in (45 x 19 mm)	8 ft 9 in (2660 mm)
Hardwood/softwood for drawer guides, 2	$\frac{3}{4}$ x $\frac{3}{4}$ in (19 x 19 mm)	4 ft $4\frac{1}{2}$ in (1330 mm)
Hardwood/softwood for drawer runner blocks, 2	1 x $\frac{7}{8}$ in (25 x 21 mm)	$6\frac{1}{4}$ in (160 mm)
Hardwood/softwood for drawer front, 1	$3\frac{1}{2}$ x $\frac{3}{4}$ in (90 x 19 mm)	1 ft 8 in (510 mm)
Hardwood/softwood for drawer sides, 2	$3\frac{1}{2}$ x $\frac{5}{8}$ in (90 x 16 mm)	4 ft 8 in (1420 mm)
Hardwood/softwood for drawer back, 1	$2\frac{7}{8}$ x $\frac{5}{8}$ in (72 x 16 mm)	1 ft 8 in (510 mm)
Hardwood/softwood for drawer bottom, 1	1 ft $8\frac{1}{2}$ in x $\frac{3}{8}$ in (521 x 10 mm)	2 ft $4\frac{3}{8}$ in (721 mm)
Plywood for tongues, 4	$\frac{1}{4}$ x $\frac{1}{4}$ in (6 x 6 mm)	3 in (75 mm)
Drawer knob, 1		
No. 20 beech biscuits		
Fluted beech dowels	$\frac{5}{16}$ in (8 mm)	
Brass right-angled stretcher plates, 10		
Woodscrews		

PLATE DISPLAY UNIT

This decorative softwood plate rack can be adapted easily to suit the available space in any kitchen. The frame uses through mortise-and-tenon joints, glued and wedged in place, and the three drawers add storage room.

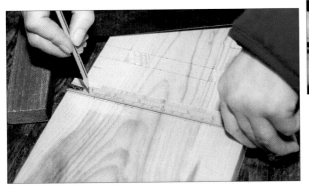

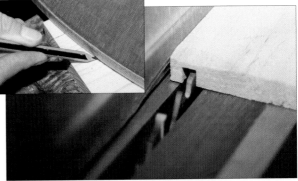

1 Cut the sides, shelves and drawer dividers. Mark and cut the eight mortise holes on each side to 1 in (25 mm) wide and ¾ in (19 mm) high. Cut the tenon shoulders on the drawer dividers and the matching mortises on the bottom two shelves. Cut the tenons on the ends of the shelves to match the mortises in the sides, adding two saw cuts toward the edges of each tenon for the wedges. Dry-assemble the frame; don't worry if the shelf tenons seem a little loose in the sides, as they will be tightened by the wedges.

2 Mark and cut a ¼-in (6-mm) wide groove along the top of the two middle shelves, to hold plates – this can be just in front of the middle or further toward the front, as you require. Cut the groove using a router and rounded carving cutter, or a grooving plane, or even two saw cuts. Or, you can cut, glue, and nail on a length of ¼ x ¼ in (6 x 6 mm) wood. Mark out the curves on the sides to your preferred profile – this project used a bucket for the top and bottom curves – then cut the curves and clean them up (see inset).

3 Mark and cut the bearer to 2 ft ¼ in (612 mm), and drill a central hole, to be used for fixing the rack to a wall. Mark and cut a matching ⅞ x ¾ in (21 x 19 mm) stopped half-dado joint in the inside back of the sides, and a same-size half-dado in the back of the drawer dividers. Clean and sand all the parts.

4 Apply glue to the frame joints and clamp using bar clamps and checking for square. Cut wedges for the tenons from the side offcuts, and drive them home gently but firmly, using a mallet. Wipe off any glue that is squeezed out. Glue and screw the bearer into the half-dado joints at the back.

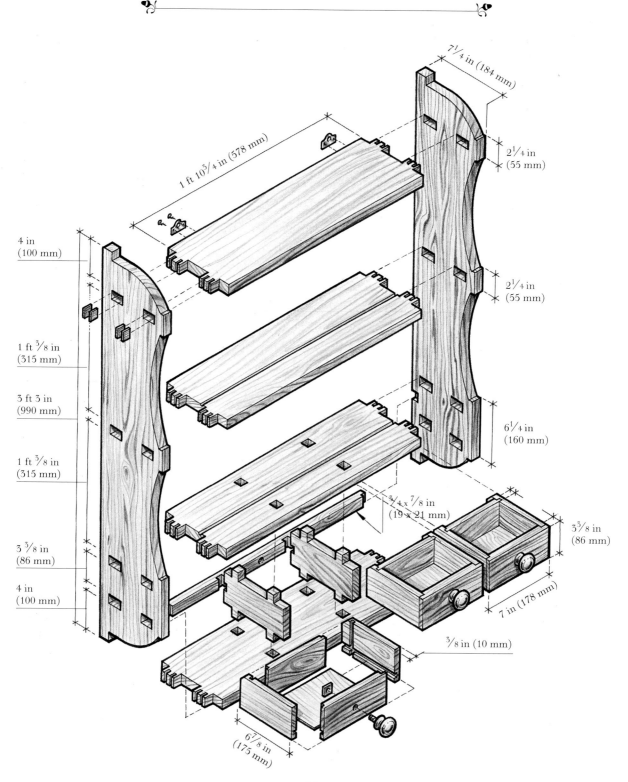

7 1/4 in (184 mm)

1 ft 10 3/4 in (578 mm)

2 1/4 in (55 mm)

4 in (100 mm)

2 1/4 in (55 mm)

1 ft 3/8 in (315 mm)

3 ft 3 in (990 mm)

6 1/4 in (160 mm)

1 ft 3/8 in (315 mm)

3/4 x 7/8 in (19 x 21 mm)

3 3/8 in (86 mm)

3 3/8 in (86 mm)

7 in (178 mm)

4 in (100 mm)

3/8 in (10 mm)

6 7/8 in (175 mm)

5 Mark and cut the drawer fronts to 7 in (178 mm) length, drawer sides and bottoms to 6⁷/₈ in (175 mm), and the drawer backs to 6³/₄ in (170 mm). Cut dado joints at each end of the fronts for the sides, and cut half-dado joints in the backs and matching grooves in the rear of the sides. Cut a ¹/₄ in (6 mm) groove above the bottom edge of the front and sides, to fit the bottoms. Dry-assemble the drawers, then apply glue to the frame joints and nail them in place, checking for square. When dry, push the bottoms into place along the grooves and nail them in position.

6 Drill a ¹/₈ in (4 mm) central hole in each drawer front, then clean and sand the drawers. After finishing, fit the brass knobs to the drawers and the hooks to the undersides of the top two and the bottom shelves – check the size of cups or mugs before making the guide marks for the hooks.

LIST OF MATERIALS *(measurements indicate cut size)*

ITEM	SECTION	LENGTH
Softwood for sides, 2	7¹/₄ x ³/₄ in (184 x 19 mm)	6 ft 6 in (1980 mm
Softwood for shelves, 4	7¹/₄ x ³/₄ in (184 x 19 mm)	8 ft 1 in (2464 mm)
Softwood for drawer dividers, 2	5 x ³/₄ in (125 x 19 mm)	1 ft 2¹/₂ in (368 mm)
Softwood for drawer fronts, 3	3³/₈ x ³/₄ in (86 x 19 mm)	1 ft 9 in (534 mm)
Softwood for drawer sides, 6	6³/₈ x ³/₈ in (162 x 10 mm)	3 ft 5¹/₄ in (1050 mm)
Softwood for drawer backs, 3	3¹/₈ x ³/₈ in (80 x 10 mm)	1 ft 8¹/₄ in (510 mm)
Softwood for drawer bottoms, 3	6¹/₂ x ¹/₄ in (165 x 6 mm)	1 ft 8⁵/₈ in (525 mm)
Softwood for bearer, 1	⁷/₈ x ³/₄ in (21 x 19 mm)	2 ft ¹/₄ in (612 mm)
Woodscrews, 4, and panel nails		
Brass knobs, 3, and hooks, 10		
Brass hanging plates, 2		

LIMED CUPBOARD

This cupboard is designed to fit on top of an existing work top. It uses blockboard faced with limed-oak veneer for the cupboard carcasses, softwood for the drawer carcasses, and solid oak for the carcass frames, drawer fronts and doors. The drawer carcasses are made using traditional dovetail joints.

1 Cut the carcass sides to 4 ft 3¼ in (1302 mm), and cut ¾-in (19-mm) dado joints flush with the top and bottom and 6¾ in (170 mm) from the bottom, to take the fixed shelves. Cut the fixed shelves to 1 ft 6½ in (470 mm). To assemble the carcass, drill pilot holes and screw the fixed shelves into place through the sides.

2 Cut the four vertical frames to 4 ft 3⅝ in (1311 mm), and the four horizontal frames to 1 ft 5¾ in (451 mm), and route a small decorative molding into all the front edges. Cut a 45° chamfer across the ends of the moldings on the horizontal frames, and cut and chamfer a length of beading on the vertical pieces to match. Drill pilot holes through the top and bottom of the sides, and screw the frames together.

3 Cut the door stiles to 3 ft 4⅝ in (1032 mm), and use a router to cut the moldings and the grooves. Set the stiles out to give the correct width for the doors, then cut the rails to 1 ft 1⅜ in (340 mm). Because the doors are to be fitted with glass, use a circular saw to turn the groove cut by the router into a rabbet.

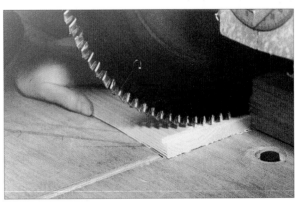

4 Scribe the ends of the rails, using a router and trimmer. Dry-assemble the stiles and rails: if there is a small gap, fill it in later, using ¼ in (6 mm) strips of wood. Cut the moldings on the rails.

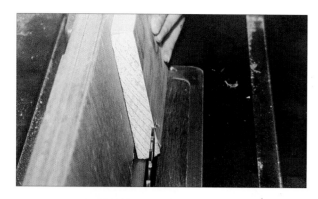

5 Cut the four horizontal glazing bars to 1 ft 1⅜ in (340 mm), and the six vertical ones to 11¾ in (300 mm). Cut the rabbets on a table saw or router, then cut the moldings on a router. Cut the ¼ in (6 mm) 'tenons' on the ends of the horizontal glazing bars and the appropriate vertical glazing bars, then apply glue to the joints and assemble the doors. Clean out the rabbets and seal with shellac before running putty for the glass. Cut and glue or nail the molding into place.

6 Trim the doors to fit the frames, then cut slots for the biscuits in the frame backs, the front of the carcass sides, and the top and bottom shelves. Glue, insert biscuits, and clamp the frames to the carcasses. Hang the doors from the cupboard frames using three brass butt or flush hinges for each door, as shown.

7 Cut the false drawer stiles and rails. Cut a scribe and tongue on the rail ends, then cut a decorative molding on the inside edges of the stiles and rails, using a router. Cut a ¼ in (6 mm) groove to take the drawer false panels. Cut the panels to 1 ft ½ in (320 mm), and raise the edges on a spindle molder or router. Use a circular saw or router to rabbet the edges to fit into the grooves, and drill pilot holes for handles. Glue the joints and assemble false fronts.

8 Cut drawer sides to 11 in (280 mm) and fronts and backs to 1 ft 3¾ in (400 mm). Cut the backs slightly short, and cut a ⅛ in (4 mm) groove for the plywood bottoms in the sides and front. Cut ¾ in (19 mm) grooves for the drawer runners in the outer edges of the sides. Cut dovetails by hand in the sides, fronts and backs. Assemble drawers, and screw on false front and handles. Cut drawer runners to 9¾ in (250 mm), and screw to cupboard sides.

Finishing

Cover the screw holes in the outer carcass sides with oak veneer plywood cut to shape. Cut similar veneer to make the cupboard backs, and pin it in place from the back. Cover the joint between the front frame of the cupboard and the tongue and groove by gluing and pinning molding in place. To lime the cupboard unit on pages 24–25, use mineral spirits to thin special white non-drip liming filler,

then apply it enough to cover the surface. Clean the filler off with a cloth, making sure that the grain shows through – this requires a delicate touch, so practice on scrap wood first to gain confidence.

Seal the limed surfaces and the inside of the cupboards with lacquer; if you use cellulose lacquer with a brush, thin it a little and apply very lightly.

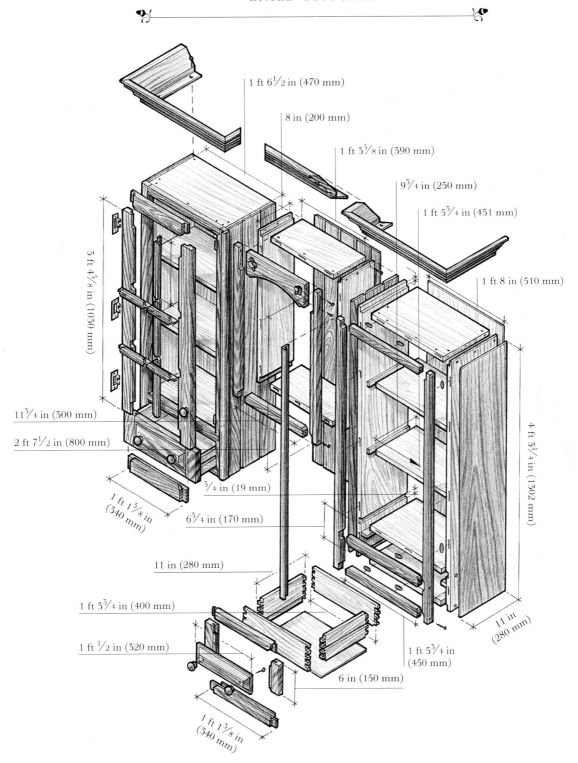

1 ft 6½ in (470 mm)

8 in (200 mm)

1 ft 3⅜ in (390 mm)

9¾ in (250 mm)

1 ft 5¾ in (451 mm)

1 ft 8 in (510 mm)

3 ft 4⅝ in (1030 mm)

11¾ in (300 mm)

2 ft 7½ in (800 mm)

4 ft 3¼ in (1302 mm)

¾ in (19 mm)

1 ft 1⅜ in (340 mm)

6¾ in (170 mm)

11 in (280 mm)

11 in (280 mm)

1 ft 3¾ in (400 mm)

1 ft ½ in (320 mm)

1 ft 5¾ in (450 mm)

6 in (150 mm)

1 ft 1⅜ in (340 mm)

9 Cut the loose shelves to 1 ft 5³⁄₄ in (451 mm), and the shelf bearers to 9³⁄₄ in (250 mm). Screw the bearers to the inside of the sides – for neatness, align them with the horizontal glazing bars in the doors. Screw the loose shelves to the bearers, and then fix magnetic catches to the tops and bottoms of the doors, and to the carcass sides.

10 You can either use pre-molded cornice pieces or machine them yourself on a spindle molder or router. Cut the cornice pieces to length, and cut the miters using a miter jig on a table saw. Cut the cornice support bearers to the appropriate lengths, and screw the cornices to the bearers. Glue and nail the cornice corners, and then fit to the carcass. The center section should be slightly narrower than the cupboards, as well as shorter and less deep.

11 Whether you use pre-molded tongue and groove for the center back and side panels, or machine it yourself on a spindle molder or router table, cut the ten boards to 4 ft 3¹⁄₄ in (1302 mm) and screw four to the back of the center section and three each to the inner sides of the carcasses. Cut the center section sides and vertical frame pieces to 2 ft 7¹⁄₂ in (800 mm) and the top and bottom pieces and center section horizontal piece to 1 ft 3³⁄₈ in (390 mm). Assemble the sides and top and bottom by screwing through the sides. Cut out a 4³⁄₄ in (120 mm) rabbet for the arch in the tops of the vertical frame pieces, assemble the frame and fix it to the sides and bottom with beech biscuits, as for the door frames.

12 Cut the arch to 1 ft 2¹⁄₂ in (370 mm), and shape it on a bandsaw or fretsaw. Make the cutouts using a drill press and coping saw. Either use a scraper plane to cut the molding on the lower edge, or cut a strip of beading to length, make small saw cuts along the back; steam-bend the beading and glue and clamp it to the arch. Glue the arch into the rabbets in the vertical frame pieces, then screw the center section in place through the cupboard carcass sides.

LIST OF MATERIALS *(measurements indicate cut size)*

ITEM	SECTION	LENGTH
CUPBOARDS		
Blockboard for carcass sides, 4, and fixed shelves, 6	11 in x $^3/_4$ in (280 x 19 mm)	26 ft 4 in (8028 mm)
Blockboard for loose shelves, 4	$9^3/_4$ in x $^3/_4$ in (250 x 19 mm)	5 ft 11 in (1804 mm)
Blockboard for center section sides, 2, top, 1, and bottom, 1	8 x $^3/_4$ in (200 x 19 mm)	7 ft $9^3/_4$ in (2380 mm)
Softwood for shelf bearers, 8	$^3/_4$ x $^3/_8$ in (19 x 10 mm)	6 ft 6 in (2000 mm)
Oak for vertical frames, 4, and center section vertical frames, 2	$1^1/_8$ x 1 in (30 x 25 mm)	22 ft $5^1/_2$ in (6844 mm)
Oak for horizontal frames, 6, center section horizontal frame, 1	$1^5/_8$ x 1 in (40 x 25 mm)	9 ft $10^1/_4$ in (3000 mm)
Oak for arch, 1	$4^3/_4$ x 1 in (120 x 25 mm)	1 ft $2^1/_2$ in (370 mm)
Oak for cornice	5 in x $3^1/_2$ in (125 x 90 mm)	11 ft $5^3/_4$ in (3495 mm)
Softwood for cornice support bearer	1 x $^3/_4$ in (25 x 19 mm)	10 ft $5^3/_4$ in (3190 mm)
Oak-veneered plywood for cupboard backs, 2	1 ft 8 in x $^1/_8$ in (510 x 4 mm)	8 ft $6^1/_2$ in (2604 mm)
Oak-veneered plywood for side coverings, 2	11 x $^1/_8$ in (280 x 4 mm)	8 ft $6^1/_2$ in (2604 mm)
Oak for center section back and side panels, 10	$4^1/_4$ x $^5/_8$ in (110 x 16 mm)	42 ft $8^1/_2$ in (13.02 m)
Softwood for drawer runners, 4, and beech biscuits	1 x $^3/_4$ in (25 x 19 mm)	3 ft 3 in (1000 mm)
DOORS		
Oak for rails, 4, and stiles, 4	$2^1/_2$ x 1 in (65 x 25 mm)	18 ft (5488 mm)
Oak for glazing bars, 10	1 x 1 in (25 x 25 mm)	10 ft 4 in (3160 mm)
Beading for glass		
DRAWERS		
Oak for false front rails, 4	$1^1/_8$ x 1 in (30 x 25 mm)	4 ft $5^1/_2$ in (1360 mm)
Oak for false front stiles, 4	$2^1/_2$ x 1 in (65 x 25 mm)	2 ft (610 mm)
Oak for false front panels, 2	$4^1/_4$ x 1 in (110 x 25 mm)	2 ft 1 in (635 mm)
Softwood for drawer sides, 4, fronts, 2, and backs, 2	$4^3/_4$ x $^5/_8$ in (120 x 16 mm)	8 ft 11 in (2720 mm)
Plywood for bottoms, 2	11 x $^1/_8$ in (280 x 4 mm)	2 ft $7^1/_2$ in (805 mm)
Oak knobs or handles, 6, brass butts or flush hinges, 6		
Magnetic catches, 4, woodscrews		

WHEELBACK KITCHEN CHAIR

The classic design of these chairs has made
them kitchen favorites for many decades.
They were traditionally made from a variety
of woods, with elm, beech, yew, and
ash often being used in the same chair.
The construction involves steam-bending
and turning, although you can buy
ready-turned components.

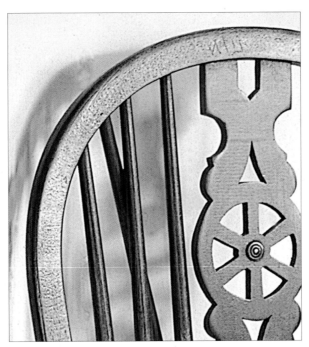

The round sticks are tapered at the top.

1 Make up the width of the seat, if necessary, by gluing strips of timber together and cutting matching dovetails on the underside. Use a template to cut the seat to shape, and shape the top with an adze, varying the width between 1⁵/₈ in (40 mm) at the widest edges and just over ³/₄ in (19 mm). Finish the carving of the seat top with a small thumb plane and a scraper. Cut the legs to 1ft 5⁷/₈ in (457 mm) length, then turn each blank to a bobbin before building up the features using gouges and skew chisels. Trim down the tops of the legs to 1 in (25 mm) diameter, using a rounding-off tool. Cut the two side stretchers to 1 ft 2⁷/₈ in (377 mm) and the center stretcher to 1 ft 4³/₈ in (415 mm), and turn them to shape.

2 Hold the seat in the vice, with the bottom facing out, and level the marks for the holes for the back pair of legs to the line of the bench top. Clamp a sheet of plywood to a trestle and align its top edge exactly with the centers of the holes and the bench top. Take the angles of splay from the illustration and mark the offsets to the side; you can also use an angle bevel to mark the splay. Drill the holes to 1 in (25 mm) diameter, but do not drill through the seat. Fit the legs to the seat, then use a straightedge and two hand clamps to establish the position for the side stretchers.

3 Mark the sides of the legs to establish the angles of the side stretcher holes, and sight down the legs from above to mark the center point. Drill the holes, trim the stretchers to length and push them into place: insert the front leg, insert the stretcher and then press the back leg into position, locating the stretcher as you do. Mark the position and angles for the center stretcher, drill the holes in the side stretchers, and fit the center stretcher. Mark each component with its correct orientation and number each part. It is also worth marking a depth line on each leg before disassembling, applying glue and reassembling.

4 Cut the back bow to 4 ft 1 in (1240 mm) length and plane it to ¹/₁₆ in (1.6 mm) oversize. Steam it in a small steam chest for at least 2 hours. Remove and clamp it in a former to a tighter radius than the finished curve, to allow for any spring back when the wood is released. The former shown here uses a galvanized iron strap with elm blocks bolted to it by roofing bolts, and ring bolts at each end.

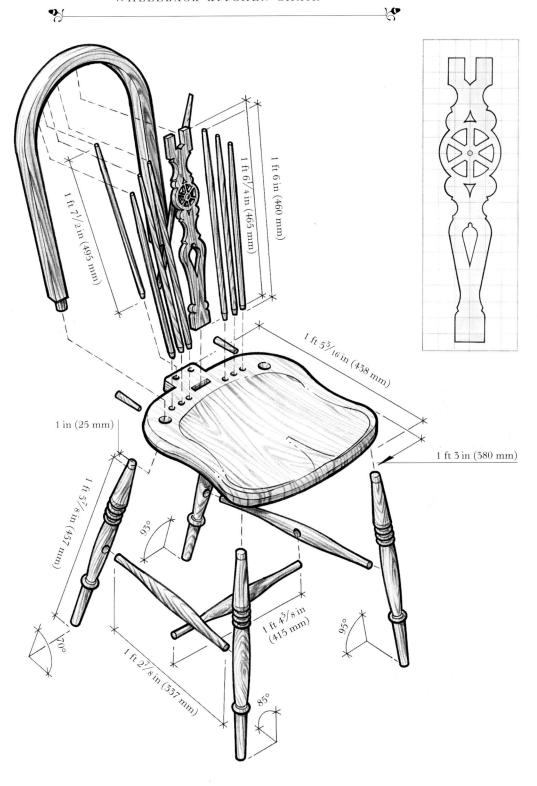

1 ft 7¹/₂ in (495 mm)

1 ft 6¹/₄ in (465 mm)

1 ft 6 in (460 mm)

1 ft 5³/₁₆ in (438 mm)

1 in (25 mm)

1 ft 3 in (380 mm)

1 ft 5⁷/₈ in (457 mm)

95°

1 ft 4³/₈ in (415 mm)

70°

1 ft 2⁷/₈ in (337 mm)

95°

85°

5 Mark the positions of the 1 in (25 mm) diameter holes for the back bow on the top of the seat. Make up two simple guides for the angles of splay (see the diagram on page 33) – one for the backward slope of the bow, and the other for the angle to the side. Clamp them to the seat, and use them to determine the angle of the drill for each hole. Drill right through the seat. When the back bow has set to the correct curve, release it from the former and plane the front surface smooth, then clamp it in the vice and cut the radius on the back curve with a spokeshave. Finish the shaping with a chair scraper. To add decoration, make up a gauge using a screw and block of wood, and run it around the back of the bow (see inset).

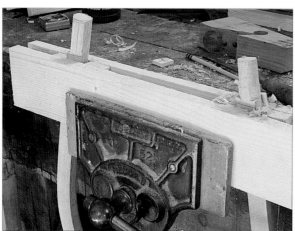

6 Clamp the ends of the back bow in a vice or simple jig, and mark the length of the cylinder shape to fit into the seat holes. Make a template for the circumference by drilling a 1 in (25 mm) hole in plywood, then saw off the corners of the bow ends and chisel them to form the cylinder shape, finishing with the rounding-off tool used for the legs. Push the bow in the seat holes. Use dividers to scribe the finished trim line around each end, remove the bow and cut back to the line with a chisel and fine saw. Replace the bow in the seat, push into place again, and mark the level of the seat underside on the raised stub. Remove the bow and drill a $\frac{1}{4}$ in (6 mm) hole through the stubs, centered on the line, and prepare tapering dowels to hold the bow down firmly in place.

7 Replace the bow, and mark the positions of the sticks and splat on the seat and on the front face of the bow. Mark and cut out the splat, using a fretsaw or a jigsaw fitted with a fine blade, and cut out the decorative wheel and other holes. Remove the bow and drill the holes for the sticks in the seat as shown here, using a $\frac{5}{8}$ in (16 mm) auger bit. Mark off the mortises for the splat, drill out the waste with a $\frac{3}{8}$ in (10 mm) bit, and finish up using a mallet and chisel.

8 Mark the center point for each stick hole on the bow, then clamp it in a vice and drill the holes; for the acute angles of the V-sticks, start with the drill perpendicular to the wood, then swing the drill to the correct angle. Mark the outline of the mortises for the splat, using a gauge, then drill out the waste and finish with a chisel. Fit the splat into the seat, then slip the bow into position and adjust the splat to length until the bow can be driven in completely. Use the tapered pegs to hold the bow in place.

9 Cut the sticks slightly overlength: the two V-sticks to 1 ft $7\frac{1}{2}$ in (495 mm), and the six shorter ones to 1 ft 6 in (460 mm). Use an offcut of wood as a measuring stick, then cut the six shorter sticks about $\frac{1}{8}$ in (4 mm) short, and the V-sticks exactly to length. Taper the top third of each stick, using a shoulder plane and scraper, and finish with sandpaper so the end diameter is just less than $\frac{3}{8}$ in (10 mm). Carve a small taper at the bottom end of each step.

10 Dry-assemble the sticks, splat, and bow. Adjust, then disassemble; run glue into the seat holes and bow, and reassemble. Pull the bow hard down to the seat and hold it with the tapered pegs until dry. Drill a $\frac{1}{4}$ in (6 mm) hole through the outside edge of the seat and the bottoms of the bow, and glue in hardwood dowels to hold the bow. Saw off the bow stubs, and lightly sand the chair. Fit a small roundel into the center splat wheel.

LIST OF MATERIALS *(measurements indicate cut size)*

ITEM	SECTION	LENGTH
Hardwood/softwood for seat, 1	1 ft 3 in x $1\frac{5}{8}$ in (380 x 40 mm)	1 ft $5\frac{3}{16}$ in (438 mm)
Hardwood/softwood for legs, 4	$1\frac{3}{4}$ in (45 mm) diameter	5 ft $11\frac{1}{2}$ in (1828 mm)
Hardwood/softwood for side stretchers, 2, and center stretcher, 1	$1\frac{1}{8}$ in (30 mm) diameter	3 ft $10\frac{1}{8}$ in (1169 mm)
Hardwood/softwood for splat, 1	$4\frac{1}{8}$ x $\frac{3}{8}$ in (105 x 10 mm)	1 ft $6\frac{1}{4}$ in (465 mm)
Hardwood/softwood for back bow, 1	$1\frac{1}{4}$ x $1\frac{1}{8}$ in (32 x 30 mm)	4 ft 1 in (1240 mm)
Hardwood/softwood for sticks, 8, and roundel	$\frac{5}{8}$ in (16 mm) diameter	12 ft $3\frac{3}{8}$ in (3760 mm)

SPICE CABINET

This little box, based on a 19th-century spice cabinet, uses dovetail, halving, and stopped dado joints in its construction. Using quarter-sawn oak reduces the possibility of the thin boards warping, but any hardwood will work well.

1 Mark and cut the top and bottom to $7\frac{1}{4}$ in (184 mm). Cut a $\frac{1}{8}$ in (4 mm) rabbet along the inside back edge of the sides, then cut to $5\frac{3}{8}$ in (137 mm) length. Mark the $\frac{3}{16}$ in (5 mm) square stopped housings for the rails to $\frac{1}{4}$ in (6 mm) from the front edge in the sides, then cut and clean them up. Cut a matching $\frac{1}{4}$ in (6 mm) notch in the front edges of the sides, and trim to fit.

2 Mark the halving joints in the rails and the center division piece to half their width – $1\frac{1}{2}$ in (38 mm) – then cut them out with a tenon saw and remove the waste with a chisel. Dry-assemble the sides, rails and center division, checking that they are square with a steel ruler. Plane any surfaces that do not align.

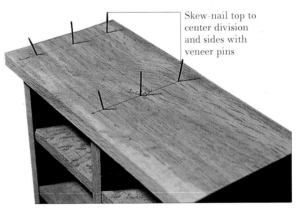

Skew-nail top to center division and sides with veneer pins

3 Mark the dovetail housing for the center division in the top, to stop $\frac{1}{4}$ in (6 mm) from the front edge. Cut it $\frac{1}{8}$ in (4 mm) deep, first as a narrow, $\frac{1}{8}$-in (4-mm) square-bottomed slot, using the point of a dovetail saw and a chisel, then use a bevel-edged chisel to make it into a dovetail housing, $\frac{3}{16}$ in (5 mm) wide at the bottom. Cut a matching dovetail in the top edge of the center division, using a bevel-edged chisel. Dry-assemble the joint as you go (see inset).

4 Apply glue to the halving joint in the rails and center division and push them together. Slot the rails into the stopped housings in the sides and slide the top into position. Skew-nail the top to the sides and center division, using veneer pins, and position the bottom and skew-nail it to the sides and center division. Before cutting the drawer components to length, cut a $\frac{1}{8}$ in (4 mm) groove $\frac{1}{8}$ in (4 mm) from the bottom of the inside edges of the front and sides.

7¹/₄ in (184 mm)

3³/₈ in (86 mm)

80 mm (3¹/₈ in)

5³/₈ in (137 mm)

³/₁₆ in (5 mm)

⁵/₁₆ in (8 mm)

1⁵/₈ in (40 mm)

2⁷/₈ in (72 mm)

⁵/₁₆ in (8 mm)

3 in (75 mm)

Finishing

Only the outside of the carcass, the inside of the top and the drawer fronts and top edges need to be finished, although you can apply finish to other surfaces. To create an aged brown, warm a little linseed oil and oil varnish in separate basins of water; when they are both very hot, add the oil to the varnish in a proportion of 1 part oil to 3 parts varnish. Next, add in brown umber and a little alizarin crimson oil paint and stir and shake until it is in suspension. Brush on the mixture while it is still warm, wiping off any oily residue. Let dry overnight, then wax the cabinet with brown wax.

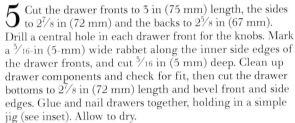

5 Cut the drawer fronts to 3 in (75 mm) length, the sides
to $2^{7}/_{8}$ in (72 mm) and the backs to $2^{5}/_{8}$ in (67 mm).
Drill a central hole in each drawer front for the knobs. Mark
a $^{3}/_{16}$-in (5-mm) wide rabbet along the inner side edges of
the drawer fronts, and cut $^{3}/_{16}$ in (5 mm) deep. Clean up
drawer components and check for fit, then cut the drawer
bottoms to $2^{7}/_{8}$ in (72 mm) length and bevel front and side
edges. Glue and nail drawers together, holding in a simple
jig (see inset). Allow to dry.

6 Drive home the nails and fit the drawers into the
carcass. Sand the cabinet front, then use a rabbet plane
and sandpaper to round off the edges of the top. Drive the
nails in the top well below the surface, then whittle
wooden pegs to fit the holes and glue in place. Fit the
knobs to the drawer fronts after finishing.

LIST OF MATERIALS *(measurements indicate cut size)*		
ITEM	SECTION	LENGTH
Hardwood for top, 1, and bottom, 1	$3^{3}/_{8}$ x $^{5}/_{16}$ in (86 x 8 mm)	1 ft $2^{1}/_{2}$ in (368 mm)
Hardwood for sides, 2	$3^{1}/_{8}$ x $^{5}/_{16}$ in (80 x 8 mm)	$10^{3}/_{4}$ in (274 mm)
Hardwood for rails, 2, and center division, 1	3 x $^{3}/_{16}$ in (75 x 5 mm)	1 ft $7^{7}/_{8}$ in (505 mm)
Hardwood or plywood for back, 1	$5^{3}/_{8}$ x $^{1}/_{8}$ in (137 x 4 mm)	$6^{3}/_{8}$ in (162 mm)
Hardwood for drawer sides, 12	$1^{5}/_{8}$ x $^{3}/_{16}$ in (40 x 5 mm)	2 ft $10^{1}/_{2}$ in (864 mm)
Hardwood for drawer fronts, 6	$1^{5}/_{8}$ x $^{5}/_{16}$ in (40 x 8 mm)	1 ft 6 in (450 mm)
Hardwood for drawer backs, 6	$1^{1}/_{8}$ x $^{5}/_{16}$ in (30 x 8 mm)	1 ft $3^{3}/_{4}$ in (402 mm)
Hardwood or plywood for drawer bottoms, 6	$2^{7}/_{8}$ x $^{1}/_{8}$ in (72 x 4 mm)	1 ft $5^{1}/_{4}$ in (432 mm)
Hardwood for drawer knobs, 6 (or brass knobs)	$^{3}/_{8}$ in (10 mm) diameter	$3^{3}/_{4}$ in (95 mm)
Veneer nails and wooden pegs		

COUNTRY KITCHEN TABLE

This simple, classic design uses haunched mortise-and-tenon joints, with dowels for added strength, in its construction. The proportions can be altered to fit a particular space, but take care that the dimensions match any changes.

The top is secured by softwood "buttons".

1 To check that the frame is level, make a measuring rod from scrap softwood. On it mark the overall design, the position in from the table top edges of the legs, their width and the rail lengths for the long side and short end rails: on one side mark the end rail length of 1 ft 5½ in (445 mm), on the other the side rail length of 2 ft 10 in (865 mm). Use ready-turned legs, or turn them to 2¾ in (70 mm) square. Cut the legs to slightly over the finished length of 2 ft 2½ in (673 mm), to allow for damage. Cut and plane the four rails to the finished lengths. For speed use a radial arm saw, with a stop made from an offcut and held in place with a quick-release clamp.

2 Offer the rails to the leg tops to start the marking stage. Leaving a little extra space at the top of the table leg to prevent damage while working, mark off the rail widths and the 1 in (25 mm) haunched mortise at the top, as shown.

3 Using a power mortiser or hand tools, cut the 1¾-in (45-mm) deep mortises for the side and end rails in the legs, with an upper haunched section ⅝ in (16 mm) deep. Next, cut the 1½ in (38 mm) tenons on both ends of the rails, using a tenon saw, router and jig, or spindle molder. Use a right-angled piece of plywood as a template to draw the haunched sections on each tenon.

4 Cut the haunches on the tenons, then use a router or grooving saw in a spindle molder to cut a ⅜ in (10 mm) groove along the upper inside edge of each rail, to finish ¾ in (19 mm) from the top edge.

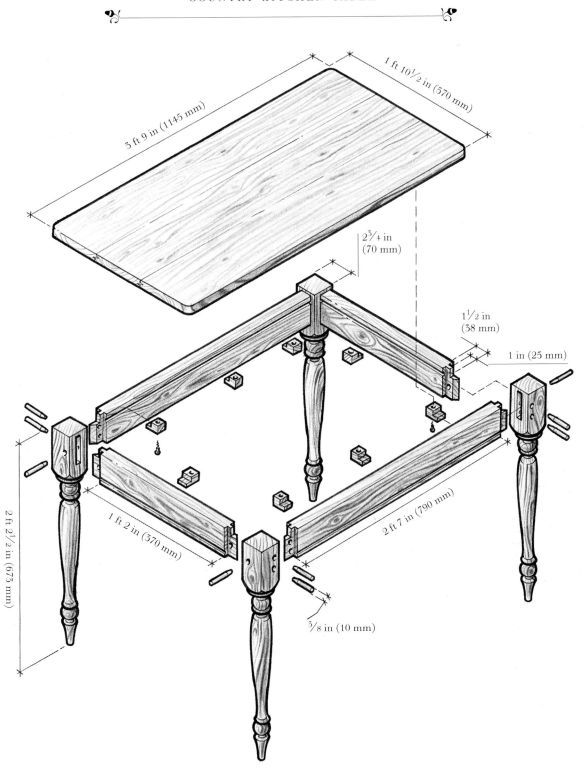

3 ft 9 in (1145 mm)

1 ft 10½ in (570 mm)

2¾ in (70 mm)

1½ in (38 mm)

1 in (25 mm)

2 ft 2½ in (673 mm)

1 ft 2 in (370 mm)

2 ft 7 in (790 mm)

⅜ in (10 mm)

5 Use a router or a molding plane to cut a small decorative molding along the bottom outside edge of each rail as shown. Because the tenons meet in the middle of the legs, mark and then cut a full-width miter across each rail tenon, using a chop saw or a miter saw.

6 Mark and bore two ³⁄₈ in (10 mm) dowel holes for the side rails in the top of each leg, and one for each end rail. As soon as the drill tip emerges from the other side of the wood, turn the piece over and finish drilling from the other side, to avoid splits. Dry-assemble the frame, numbering each joint component on the inside, then drill dowel holes through the tenons of all the rails.

7 Cut eight ³⁄₈ in (10 mm) diameter dowels to length, and chamfer on half of the ends, to allow the dowel to align with the tenon hole and pull the joint together when it reaches the other side of the leg. Glue up all the joints with PVA glue, hammer in all the dowels and clamp with bar clamps, checking for square.

8 Cut the boards for the table top to 3 ft 9 in (1145 mm), and mold a jointing profile to the inner faces. Apply glue to the molded groove line, then lay the boards with the growth rings facing alternate ways and clamp them, using bar clamps and softwood packing pieces. Remove excess glue with a chisel before it has hardened. Round the table top corners with a paint-can template and a jigsaw, then sand the top with a belt and orbital sander, finishing the edge joints with a cabinet scraper. Finally, cut the waste wood from the tops of the legs and sand smooth. Center the top on the frame. Cut eight softwood buttons to 2 in (50 mm) length and then cut a $^{3}/_{8}$ in (10 mm) "tenon" to fit the groove in the rails. Evenly position three buttons along each side and one centrally at each end, and screw them to the underside of the table top.

LIST OF MATERIALS *(measurements indicate cut size)*

ITEM	SECTION	LENGTH
Softwood for top, 1	1 ft 10$^{1}/_{2}$ in x 1 in (570 x 25 mm)	3 ft 9 in (1145 mm)
Softwood for legs, 4	2$^{3}/_{4}$ x 2$^{3}/_{4}$ in (70 x 70 mm)	8 ft 10 in (2690 mm)
Softwood for end rails, 2, and side rails, 2	3 x 1 in (75 x 25 mm)	9 ft 7 in (2925 mm)
Softwood for fixing buttons, 8	1 x $^{3}/_{4}$ in (25 x 19 mm)	1 ft 4 in (400 mm)
Softwood dowels	$^{3}/_{8}$ in (10 mm) diameter	
Woodscrews, 8		

Choosing the Height and Leveling a Table

Although many people think they are higher, nearly all Victorian and Edwardian kitchen tables — on which this design is based — are about 2 ft 6 in (760 mm) high. Before settling on the height given here, remember that chairs have to fit under the rails and not the top, and, if necessary, adjust the length of the legs accordingly.

Your table may wobble when you have finished making it, despite cutting the legs to the exact same lengths and checking everything for square. To rectify this first add packing under the short leg or legs, use a pair of compasses to mark around each leg from ground level and then cut along this line.

KITCHEN WALL UNIT

This wall-hung pine kitchen cabinet is based on a Shaker piece, and uses mortise-and-tenon and dowel joints in its construction. You can make your own adaptations – for instance, groove the upper edge of the central shelf to display plates.

The shelf heights are adjustable.

47

1 Mark and cut the components for the carcass: the top and base to 4 ft 6 in (1371 mm), the sides to 1 ft 11¾ in (602 mm), the internal sides to 1 ft 9¾ in (552 mm), the outer cross panels to 1 ft 3 in (380 mm), the central cross panel to 1 ft 8⅝ in (523 mm), the cupboard shelves to 1 ft 2¹⁵⁄₁₆ in (379 mm), and the middle shelf to 1 ft 8⁹⁄₁₆ in (522 mm). If necessary, make up the panels by gluing and butt-jointing together. Clean up all the edges with a jack plane, check for square, and use a piece of scrap wood as a measuring stick for marking the joints to make up the carcass.

2 Mark and drill three ⁵⁄₁₆ in (8 mm) dowel holes for each butt joint – in the ends of the top and base, internal sides and three cross panels, and in the matching edges of the sides. Use a drill bit with a spur top for a clean hole. Cut ⁵⁄₁₆ in (8 mm) fluted hardwood dowels for assembly and ¼ in (6 mm) dowels for dry-assembly. Next, mark and cut a ⅝ x ½ in (16 x 12 mm) rabbet for the plywood and tongue-and-groove backs along the back edge of the top, base and outer sides – use a router and rabbeting bit or a rabbet plane. Plane the inner sides and cross panels to be slightly narrower, so that the backs and tongue-and-groove panels butt up to them.

3 Mark and cut the two plywood backs and six tongue-and-groove panels to 1 ft 10¾ in (578 mm). Glue and clamp the tongue-and-groove panels, and plane the edges smooth when dry. Dry-assemble the whole carcass using the undersize dowels, hold with bar clamps and check for square, making any adjustments required. Check the measurements for the shelves, doors and drawers, then disassemble the carcass.

4 Cut the door stiles to 1 ft 5⅜ in (441 mm) and the rails to 1 ft 2 in (356 mm). Cut a rabbet in the back inner edge for the door panels, and use a router to cut a small stopped round-over profile on the front inner edges. Cut a stopped haunched tenon on each end of the rails, and a matching mortise in the stiles, then miter the meeting edges. Glue and assemble the door frames, hold with bar clamps and check for square.

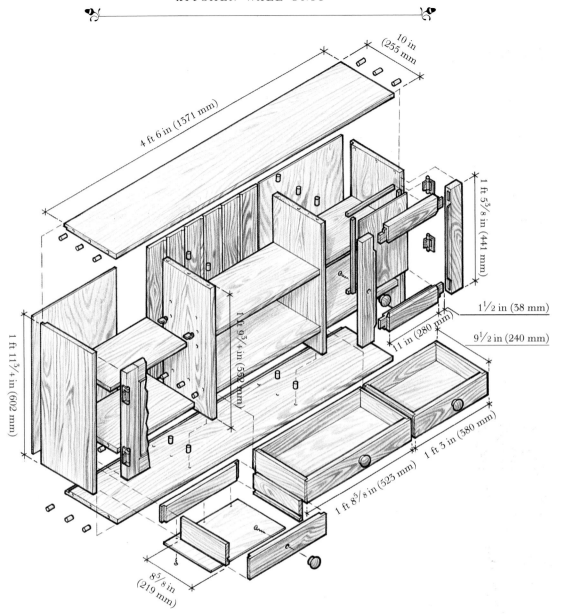

4 ft 6 in (1371 mm)

10 in (255 mm)

1 ft 5³/₈ in (441 mm)

1 ft 9³/₄ in (552 mm)

1 ft 11³/₄ in (602 mm)

1¹/₂ in (38 mm)

11 in (280 mm)

9¹/₂ in (240 mm)

1 ft 3 in (380 mm)

1 ft 8⁵/₈ in (523 mm)

8⁵/₈ in (219 mm)

Finishing

A cabinet of this sort can be finished in a number of ways; whichever you choose, it is a good idea to sand the whole piece with progressively finer grit sandpapers, ending up with 400-grit. For a pale finish that brings out the character of the pine, just use finishing oil or a clear varnish; you can stain the cabinet to match other furniture in the room (but remember to stain the door panels before assembly) and then oil or varnish it, or perhaps use a colored varnish to darken or tint it. If the grain of the wood is not very interesting, consider painting the cabinet with milk or casein paints for a traditional finish.

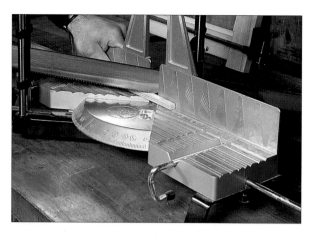

5 Mark and cut or make up the door panels to 1 ft 1¼ in (335 mm). If you are staining the cabinet, apply the stain to the panels before fitting them in place, to prevent white lines showing if the panels shrink after assembly. Drop the panels into the rabbets in the door frames, then miter-cut the beading and pin it to hold the panels in place. Drill pilot holes and fit the door knobs.

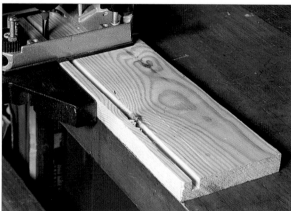

6 Cut the side drawer fronts and backs to 1 ft 3 in (380 mm), the center drawer front and back to 1 ft 8⅝ in (523 mm), and all the sides to 8⅝ in (219 mm). Cut a ¼ in (6 mm) groove along the inner face of the fronts and sides, ½ in (12 mm) up from the bottom edge, to take the drawer bottoms. Rabbet the rear end edges along the width of the fronts and the inside edges along the width of the backs to take the sides.

7 Glue and pin the drawer frames, clamp and check for square. Cut the side drawer bottoms to 1 ft 3½ in (393 mm) and the center drawer bottom to 1 ft 9⅛ in (538 mm), slide into place along the grooves and hold with screws into the bottom edge of the backs. Drill pilot holes and fit the drawer knobs, one on each side drawer, and two on the center drawer.

8 Sand all the panels and other parts using an orbital sander. Cut the six drawer stops to 2 in (50 mm) at the base and 1¼ in (32 mm) at the top, then locate them and glue and pin in place on the carcass base. Glue and assemble the carcass, and screw on the backs and tongue-and-groove panel. Mark and drill holes in the sides, and fit the brass shelf lugs. Chop out the positions of the door hinges on the side, then fit the hinges and hang the doors.

LIST OF MATERIALS *(measurements indicate cut size)*		
ITEM	SECTION	LENGTH
CARCASS		
Softwood for sides, 2, top, 1, and base, 1	10 x $\frac{3}{4}$ in (255 x 19 mm)	12 ft 11$\frac{1}{2}$ in (3946 mm)
Softwood for internal sides, 2, and cross panels, 3	9$\frac{3}{8}$ x $\frac{3}{4}$ in (238 x 19 mm)	7 ft 10$\frac{1}{8}$ in (2387 mm)
Softwood for cupboard shelves, 2	8$\frac{1}{8}$ x $\frac{3}{4}$ in (207 x 19 mm)	2 ft 5$\frac{7}{8}$ in (758 mm)
Softwood for middle shelf, 1	9$\frac{1}{2}$ x $\frac{3}{4}$ in (240 x 19 mm)	1 ft 8$\frac{9}{16}$ in (522 mm)
Plywood for cupboard backs, 2	1 ft 3$\frac{7}{8}$ in x $\frac{5}{8}$ in (403 x 16 mm)	3 ft 9$\frac{1}{2}$ in (1156 mm)
Tongue-and-groove panels for central back, 6	3$\frac{1}{2}$ x $\frac{5}{8}$ in (90 x 16 mm)	11 ft 4$\frac{1}{2}$ in (3468 mm)
Softwood for drawer stops, 6	$\frac{3}{4}$ x $\frac{3}{4}$ in (19 x 19 mm)	1 ft (305 mm)
Hardwood dowels	$\frac{5}{16}$ in (8 mm) diameter	
Brass shelf lugs, 12		
DOORS		
Softwood for stiles, 4, and rails, 4	2$\frac{1}{2}$ x $\frac{7}{8}$ in (65 x 21 mm)	10 ft 5$\frac{1}{2}$ in (3188 mm)
Softwood for panels, 2	10$\frac{3}{4}$ x $\frac{1}{4}$ in (273 x 6 mm)	2 ft 2$\frac{1}{2}$ in (670 mm)
Softwood for beading	$\frac{1}{4}$ x $\frac{1}{4}$ in (6 x 6 mm)	9 ft 1$\frac{1}{2}$ in (2790 mm)
Knobs, 2	1$\frac{3}{4}$ in (45 mm) diameter	
Brass flush hinges, 4		
DRAWERS		
Softwood for fronts, 3	3$\frac{1}{2}$ x $\frac{5}{8}$ in (90 x 16 mm)	4 ft 2$\frac{5}{8}$ in (1283 mm)
Softwood for sides, 6	3$\frac{1}{2}$ x $\frac{1}{2}$ in (90 x 12 mm)	4 ft 3$\frac{3}{4}$ in (1314 mm)
Softwood for side drawer backs, 2	2$\frac{3}{4}$ x $\frac{1}{2}$ in (70 x 12 mm)	2 ft 6 in (760 mm)
Softwood for central drawer back, 1	2$\frac{7}{8}$ x $\frac{1}{2}$ in (72 x 12 mm)	1 ft 8$\frac{5}{8}$ in (523 mm)
Plywood for bottoms, 3	9$\frac{3}{8}$ x $\frac{1}{4}$ in (238 x 6 mm)	4 ft 4$\frac{1}{8}$ in (1324 mm)
Knobs, 4	1 in (25 mm) diameter	
Woodscrews, panel nails		

OAK BREAKFRONT

Breakfronts have long been an attractive means of storage in kitchens and dining rooms. The carcass and cabinets of this breakfront are simply assembled, and the decoration on the doors, arches and cornice has a homely, country feel.

1 For the carcass, cut the sides to 2 ft 10¼ in (870 mm), the top, bottom and back to 5 ft 1 in (1550 mm), and the inner sides to 2 ft 7 in (785 mm). Cut lengths of bearer to 1 ft (305 mm), and fix the bottom to the sides via the bearer. Fit bearers at the rear of the bottom and the rear of the side panels, and screw the back to them. Screw the top in place between the sides, then cut the front kicker to 4 ft 11¾ in (1517 mm) and screw it into place between the sides, as shown.

2 Cut the cabinet sides to 3 ft 8¼ in (1123 mm), and the bottom panels, drawer shelves and tops to 1 ft 7½ in (495 mm). Use a router or radial-arm saw to cut housings in the sides for the tops, drawer shelves and bottom panels. Drill through the housings and screw the components into place, then cut the back to 5 ft 1 in (1550 mm) and screw it into position. Cut internal shelves to 1 ft 5 in (430 mm), along with their supporting bearers, but fit them after hanging the doors, so they line up with the glazing bars.

3 Cut the carcass door stiles to 2 ft 4¼ in (716 mm), the rails to 1 ft 1⅜ in (340 mm) and the muntins to 1 ft 3¼ in (385 mm). Cut cabinet door stiles to 3 ft 1 in (940 mm), the rails and the four horizontal glazing bars to 1 ft 1⅜ in (340 mm), and the six vertical glazing bars to 9¾ in (248 mm). Cut out the rabbet in the stiles for the glass or panels using a router or circular saw, then cut the mortises for all the rails and the glazing bars in the stiles.

4 On the center and bottom door rails, cut the mortises for the muntins. Cut the tenons on the rails and muntins to the rabbet line, using a radial-arm saw. To achieve an exact match between the end of the rail tenons and the molding on the stiles, use a scribing cutter in a router to scribe the end of the rail on the face.

5 Cut the molding along the edge of all the stiles and rails using a router. Using the stiles as a pattern, cut the rabbet in the back of the rails and muntins. Check the glazing bar lengths against the stiles and rails.

6 Next, dry-assemble the cabinet door frames, then cut the rabbets and edge moldings on glazing bars and fit the horizontal ones in place — tap them up and down the stile until the spacing is even. Cut the tenons in the vertical glazing bars to the rabbet line. Dry-assemble the carcass door frames, checking that the muntins fit snugly. Disassemble the doors, glue and reassemble; on the cabinet doors start with the glazing bars and work outward. Hold the doors with bar clamps, and check for square.

7 Cut the four bottom carcass door panels to 1 ft 2¼ in (360 mm) and the two top panels to 1 ft 1⅜ in (340 mm). Raise and field the panels, using a spindle molder or router — remember to machine cut the cross grain first, so that any breakout can be cleaned up when cutting with the grain. Cut the beading for the door panels to length using a miter saw, and check it for fit against the panels.

8 Use a very small drill to make the pilot holes for the panel pins, then pin the beading and panels into position. To fit the glass into the cabinet doors, run a small line of putty into the rabbet, and then miter-cut the beading and pin it into place. Drill pilot holes and screw on the door knobs. Fit brass flush hinges to the carcass and cabinets and the doors, then hang them in place. Fit the internal cabinet shelves and bearers.

9 Cut the drawer sides to 10½ in (267 mm), and the backs and fronts to 1 ft 7⅜ in (493 mm). Cut a ¼ in (6 mm) groove for the bottoms in the sides and fronts, and cut the bottoms to 1 ft 7½ in (495 mm). Assemble the drawers with dovetails, rabbets, or even butt joints, then slot the bottoms into place and hold them with glue and pins. Cut the false front stiles to 5 in (125 mm) and the rails and panels to 1 ft 1⅜ in (340 mm); make up the fronts as for the carcass doors, and screw them onto the fronts from inside. Screw on the drawer knobs.

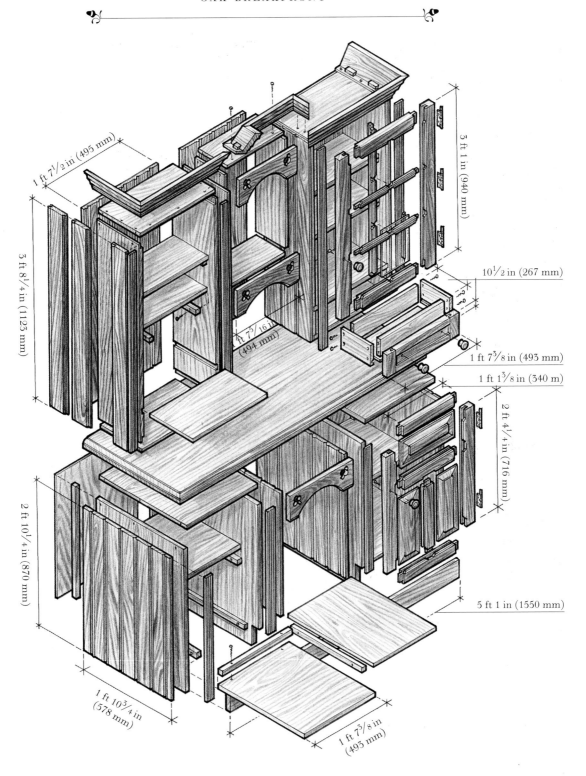

5 ft 1 in (940 mm)

1 ft 7½ in (495 mm)

10½ in (267 mm)

5 ft 8¼ in (1123 mm)

1 ft 7⁵/₁₆ in (494 mm)

1 ft 7³/₈ in (493 mm)

1 ft 1³/₈ in (340 m)

2 ft 4¼ in (716 mm)

2 ft 10¼ in (870 mm)

5 ft 1 in (1550 mm)

1 ft 10³/₄ in (578 mm)

1 ft 7³/₈ in (493 mm)

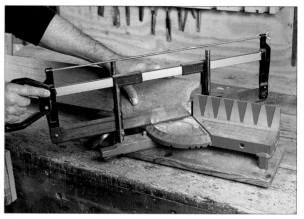

10 Cut the tongue-and-groove boards roughly to length before starting any molding. For the carcass, the lengths are 2 ft 10¼ in (870 mm) for the sides, and 2 ft 7 in (787 mm) for the inner sides and center section; for the cabinets, the sides, inner sides and center sections are all 3 ft 8¼ in (1123 mm). Cut all the grooves on one side and the tongues on the other, then add the final molding detail, such as a small bead or "V" shape. Fit the boards together and screw into place from the inside or the back. Cut the moldings for the carcass to 2 ft 5¾ in (755 mm), and for the cabinets to 3 ft 8¼ in (1123 mm); cut the profile on the faces and glue in place.

11 Cut the profile on the cornice using a spindle molder (with a router, the size will have to be reduced from the given 5 in [125 mm]). Rip a 30° angle from the top and bottom, clean up using a surface planer, then cut to the various lengths using a miter saw. Glue and nail the cornice together, and position on top of the cabinet assembly using brackets or angle pieces.

12 Cut the boards for the counter top to 5 ft 5¼ in (1657 mm) length, and fit together to make up the width using biscuit joints or tongue-and-groove joints. Clean up and ensure that the surface is flat, then run a simple molding profile around the front and sides. Drill pilot holes through the underside of the carcass top, then screw the counter top into place.

13 Cut the center section arches to 1 ft 7½ in (495 mm), and shape on a bandsaw or a jigsaw. Clean up using a spokeshave or compass plane, then rout round. Mark the cutouts using a template, and cut them out using a drill and flat bit, or a jigsaw, fretsaw or coping saw, then clean up with a file. Position the arches by screwing through the sides. Cut the cabinet center section to the same length as the arches, and fit in place.

LIST OF MATERIALS *(measurements indicate cut size)*

ITEM	SECTION	LENGTH
CARCASS		
Oak-veneered blockboard for sides, 2, top, 1, bottom, 1, and inner sides, 2	1 ft 10¾ in x ¾ in (578 x 19 mm)	21 ft ½ in (6410 mm)
Oak-veneered blockboard for front kicker, 1	3 x ¾ in (75 x 19 mm)	4 ft 11¾ in (1517 mm)
Softwood for bearers, 6	1 x 1 in (25 x 25 mm)	6 ft (1830 mm)
Oak for center section arch, 1	6 x ⅝ in (150 x 16 mm)	1 ft 7½ in (495 mm)
Plywood for back, 1	2 ft 10¼ in x ⅜ in (870 x 10 mm)	5 ft 1 in (1550 mm)
Oak tongue-and-groove boards for sides, 12, centre section, 6, and inner sides, 12	4 x ⅝ in (100 x 16 mm)	80 ft 9 in (24.6 m)
Oak for counter top, 1	1 ft 10⅞ x 1½ in (581 x 38 mm)	5 ft 5¼ in (1657 mm)
Oak for moldings, 4	¾ x ¼ in (19 x 6 mm)	9 ft 11 in (3020 mm)
CABINETS		
Oak-veneered blockboard for sides, 4, bottoms, 2, drawer shelves, 2, and tops, 2	11¾ x ¾ in (300 x 19 mm)	24 ft 6 in (7462 mm)
Oak for internal shelves, 4	10⅝ x ½ in (270 x 12 mm)	5 ft 8 in (1720 mm)
Softwood for bearers, 8	1 x 1 in (25 x 25 mm)	6 ft (1840 mm)
Oak tongue-and-groove boards for sides, 12, and backs, 18	4 x ⅝ in (100 x 16 mm)	110 ft 7½ in (33.69 m)
Oak for center section arches, 2	6 x ⅝ in (150 x 16 mm)	3 ft 3 in (990 mm)
Oak for center shelf, 1	6 x ¾ in (150 x 19 mm)	1 ft 7½ in (495 mm)
Oak for cornice	5 x 1 in (125 x 25 mm)	10 ft 3 in (3123 mm)
Plywood for back, 1	3 ft 8¼ in x ⅜ in (1123 x 10 mm)	5 ft 1 in (1550 mm)
Oak for moldings, 4	¾ x ¼ in (19 x 6 mm)	14 ft 9 in (4492 mm)
CARCASS DOORS		
Oak for stiles, 4, rails, 6, and muntins, 2	3 x 1 in (75 x 25 mm)	18 ft 7¾ in (5674 mm)
Oak for horizontal panels, 2	4 x 1 in (100 x 25 mm)	2 ft 2¾ in (680 mm)
Oak for vertical panels, 4	7 x 1 in (178 x 25 mm)	4 ft 9 in (1440 mm)
Softwood for beading	¼ x ¼ in (6 x 6 mm)	20 ft (6110 mm)
Knobs, 2	1½ in (38 mm) diameter	
Magnetic catches, 4, brass flush hinges, 4		
CABINET DOORS		
Oak for stiles, 4, and rails, 4	3 x 1 in (75 x 25 mm)	16 ft 9½ in (5120 mm)
Oak for glazing bars, 10	1 x 1 in (25 x 25 mm)	9 ft 4 in (2848 mm)
Softwood for beading	¼ x ¼ in (6 x 6 mm)	31 ft 6 in (9435 mm)
Knobs, 2	1½ in (38 mm) diameter	
Magnetic catches, 4, brass flush hinges, 4		
DRAWERS		
Oak for false front stiles, 4	3 x 1 in (75 x25 mm)	1 ft 8 in (500 mm)
Oak for false front rails, 4, and panels, 2	1¼ x 1 in (32 x 25 mm)	6 ft 8¼ in (2040 mm)
Softwood for sides, 4, and fronts, 2	4⅞ x ⅝ in (123 x 16 mm)	6 ft 8¾ in (2054 mm)
Softwood for backs, 2	4½ x ⅝ in (115 x 16 mm)	3 ft 2¾ in (986 mm)
Plywood for bottoms, 2	10⅝ x ¼ in (270 x 6 mm)	3 ft 3 in (990 mm)
Knobs, 4	1¼ in (32 mm) diameter	
Woodscrews and panel nails		

FRENCH DOORS

*French doors make a stylish addition
to any kitchen that looks out onto a conservatory
or garden. Their finished size will have
to be unique to your own frame, but the method
of construction – using haunched and paired
through-tenons – is the same.*

The rails and glazing bars are held with wedges.

1 Mark and cut the stiles 4 in (100 mm) over their finished length, to allow 2 in (50 mm) at each end for protecting the doors until they are hung. Mark and cut the rails and glazing bars to length, including the length of the through-tenons at each end; here, the tenon length is 3³⁄₄ in (95 mm).

2 Select the face side of all four stiles, clamp them together and use a try square to mark the mortises for the rails and glazing bars across them. The top rail mortises are haunched, the glazing bar mortises are the width of the bar itself – here, 1⁵⁄₈ in (40 mm) – and the lower rail mortises are paired. The actual width of the mortises is determined by the remaining width (roughly one-third) of timber after allowing for an ovolo molding on the face side, and the glazing rabbet on the other.

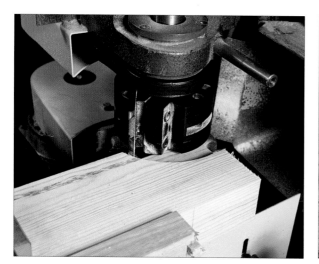

3 Use a router or spindle molder to cut the tenons. You will need a set of matched cutters to cut the shoulders of the tenons to match the moldings that will be put on the rails.

4 Cut out the central part of the tenons on the lower rails using a hand saw and a coping saw, and cut the haunches on the top rail tenons. This ensures that the corresponding mortises are not so large that they weaken the stiles.

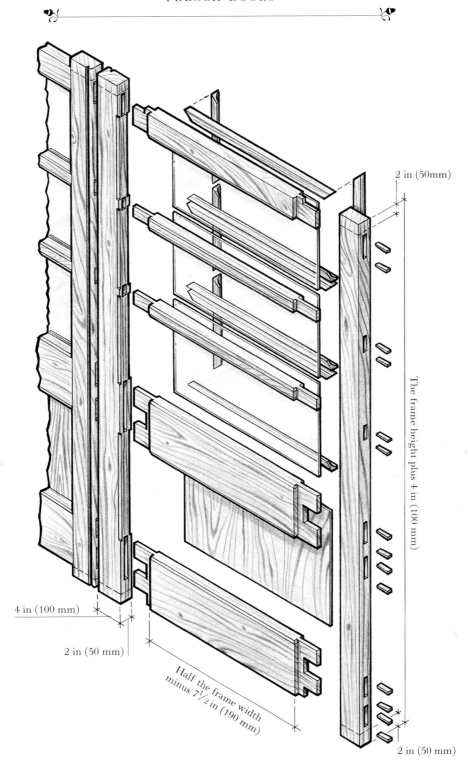

2 in (50mm)

The frame height plus 4 in (100 mm)

4 in (100 mm)

2 in (50 mm)

Half the frame width
minus 7½ in (190 mm)

2 in (50 mm)

5 Shape the moldings on all the stiles and rails using a router fitted with an ovolo cutter. On the reverse side of the stiles and rails, use a power planer to cut the $\frac{3}{8}$ x $\frac{5}{8}$ in (10 x 16 mm) glazing rabbets.

6 If you have a spindle molder, you can use this to cut the moldings and rabbets described in Step 5 in one operation.

7 Cut all the through-mortises in the stiles. The quickest method is to use a box chisel mortising machine or a box chisel in a large drill press; alternative methods are a router with a straight bit, or by hand with a chisel and mallet.

8 All the through-tenons will be wedged for stability, so use a mallet and chisel to open all the mortises in the stiles enough to drive the wedges in.

9 Dry-assemble all the components and check for fit and square, making adjustments where necessary and cleaning up the mortises. Glue under the door frames, and hold with bar clamps to keep them flat. Check again for square.

10 Drive in the wedges (here, oak was used) on either side of the tenons, clean off any excess adhesive, and allow to set. Remove the clamps and trim the wedges with a hand saw. Finish any cleaning, and sand both faces of the doors.

11 Plane the central stiles to their finished width, and cut interlocking rabbets on them. Use a router to cut a decorative molding on the inside face of one door and the outside face of the other.

12 Miter-cut the molding to length to secure the bottom panel and the glazing. Drop in the bottom panel and secure it with the molding and pins. Do not put in the glass until the frames have been painted and you are ready to trim the overlength stiles and hang the doors.

LIST OF MATERIALS (*measurements indicate cut size. No lengths are given, as each door area will have varying dimensions.*)

ITEM	SECTION
Hardwood for stiles, 4	4 x 2 in (100 x 50 mm)
Hardwood for top rails, 2	2 x 2 in (50 x 50 mm)
Hardwood for middle and bottom rails, 4	8 x 2 in (200 x 50 mm)
Hardwood for glazing bars, 4	1 1/4 x 2 in (32 x 50 mm)
Plywood for bottom panels, 2	1/2 in (12 mm)
Hardwood for wedges, 56	
Decorative molding	

SHAKER DRAWERS

This chest of drawers is based on a traditional Shaker design, with a few extras incorporated.
The carcass uses stopped mortise-and-tenon joints, and the drawers are made with dovetail joints.
Cherry is the preferred timber for the face surfaces.

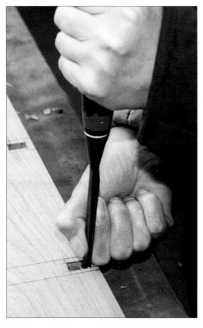

1 Mark and cut the timber for the sides to just over 3 ft 8⅝ in (1134 mm) length, then edge-join the pieces as shown, and clamp them together. When set, plane smooth and trim to size. Mark and cut a ¼ in (6 mm) rabbet along the inside back edges of both sides for the plywood back.

2 Mark and cut the eight front and two back rails to 1 ft 4⅝ in (420 mm), preferably clamped together to ensure a good shoulder line match. Mark and cut the twin stub tenons to ½ in (12 mm) depth in each end of the rails, and chop out the matching stopped mortises in the sides. Cut the top and bottom runners/kickers to 1 ft 2¼ in (360 mm) and the middle runners/kickers to 1 ft 1 in (330 mm). Mark and cut a matching ¼ in (6 mm) groove for the dust panels in the back edge of the front rails, the front edge of the back rails and the inside edges of the runners/kickers. Cut a ¼ in (6 mm) tenon on the front edges of the middle runner/kickers to join them to the front rails, and one on the back edges of the top and bottom ones.

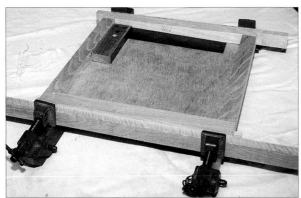

3 Cut the plywood bottom to 1 ft 2 in (356 mm) and dry-assemble it and the bottom rails, checking for square and making any adjustments. Glue and clamp up to make a framed platform construction, using bar clamps, and allow to set.

4 Dry-assemble the entire carcass – sides, platform, rails and runners/kickers – again checking for square and making any necessary alterations. When satisfied, glue and clamp up the carcass with bar clamps.

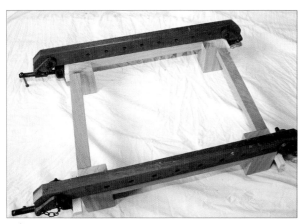

5 Cut the front and back plinth rails to 1 ft 3⅞ in (403 mm) and the side plinth rails to 1 ft 1¼ in (335 mm), and the plinth blocks to 3 in (75 mm) length. Cut twin stub tenons on each end of the plinth rails and chop out matching stopped mortises in the plinth blocks. Glue and clamp the plinth frame, checking for square. Cut the mitered front and back frame pieces to 1 ft 7¾ in (502 mm) and the mitered side frame pieces to 1 ft 5 in (430 mm), pencil around the top and bottom front edges and check that they overhang the blocks equally before gluing and screwing them into place.

6 Cut the plinth infills to 1⅛ in (30 mm), cut the profiles with a bandsaw or fretsaw, and glue to the plinth blocks and rails. Clean up and sand the plinth and carcass, and apply one coat of sanding sealer to all the visible faces. Position the plinth onto the carcass, mark and drill pilot holes, and screw the plinth to the carcass. Miter-cut the decorative scotia molding front to 1 ft 7¾ in (502 mm) and the sides to 1 ft 5 in (430 mm), and glue the whole molding in place to cover up the ledge between the plinth and the carcass (see inset).

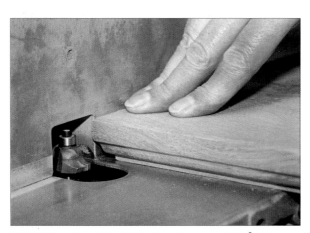

Carcass

Cabinet top

7 Mark and cut the timber for the top to 1 ft 7¾ in (502 mm) length, then edge-join the pieces and clamp them together. When set, plane smooth and round the front two corners. Using a router fitted with a bearing bit to follow the corners, cut the decorative molding on the front and side edges.

8 Fit the tenons of the runners/kickers into the grooves in the front and back rails, then mark and drill pilot holes into the sides, the holes nearest the back being slotted to allow for expansion and contraction. Position the top on the carcass, mark and drill pilot holes through the top runners/kickers and the front rail, and screw the top into place. Cut the plywood back to 3 ft 8⅝ in (1134 mm), and screw or nail it into the rabbet in the back edge of the sides.

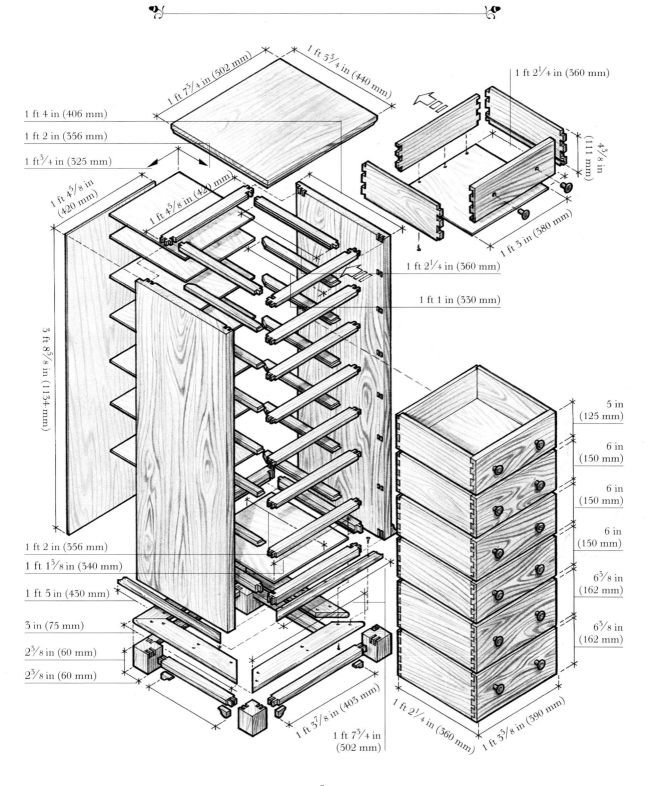

1 ft 5³/₄ in (440 mm)

1 ft 7³/₄ in (502 mm)

1 ft 2¹/₄ in (360 mm)

1 ft 4 in (406 mm)

1 ft 2 in (356 mm)

1 ft³/₄ in (325 mm)

4³/₈ in (111 mm)

1 ft 4⁵/₈ in (420 mm)

1 ft 4⁵/₈ in (420 mm)

1 ft 3 in (380 mm)

1 ft 2¹/₄ in (360 mm)

1 ft 1 in (330 mm)

3 ft 8⁵/₈ in (1134 mm)

5 in (125 mm)

6 in (150 mm)

6 in (150 mm)

6 in (150 mm)

6³/₈ in (162 mm)

1 ft 2 in (356 mm)

1 ft 1³/₈ in (340 mm)

6³/₈ in (162 mm)

1 ft 5 in (430 mm)

3 in (75 mm)

2³/₈ in (60 mm)

2³/₈ in (60 mm)

1 ft 3³/₈ in (403 mm)

1 ft 7³/₄ in (502 mm)

1 ft 2¹/₄ in (360 mm)

1 ft 3³/₈ in (390 mm)

9 Mark and cut the drawer fronts to 1 ft 3⅜ in (390 mm) and the drawer sides to 1 ft 2¼ in (360 mm). Mark and cut a ¼ in (6 mm) groove for the bottoms in all the fronts and sides. Mark out the dovetails in the fronts and sides.

10 Cut the dovetails in the fronts and sides, dry-assemble and make any adjustments necessary for a good fit. Mark and cut the drawer backs to 1 ft 3⅜ in (390 mm), and mark the dovetails with the bottom edge of the backs above the drawer. For the drawer bottoms, mark the shoulder lines on the backs a tiny amount nearer to the middle than on the fronts, to produce a slight taper on the drawers for an easy fit. Trim the top of the backs by ¼ in (6 mm), to allow for an air gap.

11 Glue and clamp the drawers, checking for square. When set, mark and cut the plywood for the drawer bottoms to 1 ft 3 in (380 mm) length, slide the bottoms into the grooves in the sides and front, and nail or screw them to the bottom edge of the backs. Test-fit the drawers into the carcass, making only fine adjustments at a time. Sand the drawers and apply sanding sealer to the fronts before drilling holes for the two knobs or handles per drawer.

LIST OF MATERIALS *(measurements indicate cut size)*		
ITEM	SECTION	LENGTH
CARCASS		
Hardwood for sides, 2	1 ft 4 in x $1\frac{1}{8}$ in (406 x 30 mm)	7 ft $5\frac{1}{4}$ in (2268 mm)
Hardwood for top front rails, 7, and top back rail, 1	$1\frac{1}{8}$ x $\frac{5}{8}$ in (30 x 16 mm)	11 ft 1 in (3360 mm)
Hardwood for bottom front rail, 1, and bottom back rail, 1	$1\frac{1}{8}$ x $1\frac{1}{16}$ in (30 x 27 mm)	2 ft $9\frac{1}{4}$ in (806 mm)
Hardwood for top, 1	1 ft $5\frac{5}{16}$ in x $1\frac{1}{8}$ in (440 x 30 mm)	1 ft $7\frac{3}{4}$ in (502 mm)
Hardwood for top runners/kickers, 2, and middle runners/kickers, 12	1 x $\frac{5}{8}$ in (25 x 16 mm)	15 ft $4\frac{1}{2}$ in (4680 mm)
Hardwood for bottom runners/kickers, 2	$1\frac{1}{16}$ x 1 in (27 x 25 mm)	2 ft $4\frac{1}{4}$ in (720 mm)
Plywood for bottom, 1	1 ft $1\frac{3}{8}$ in x $\frac{1}{4}$ in (340 x 6 mm)	1 ft 2 in (356 mm)
Plywood for dust panels, 8	1 ft $\frac{3}{4}$ in x $\frac{1}{4}$ in (325 x 6 mm)	9 ft 4 in (2840 mm)
Plywood for back, 1	1 ft $4\frac{5}{8}$ in x $\frac{1}{4}$ in (420 x 6 mm)	3 ft $8\frac{5}{8}$ in (1134 mm)
PLINTH		
Hardwood for rails, 4	$1\frac{1}{8}$ x $\frac{5}{8}$ in (30 x 16 mm)	4 ft $10\frac{1}{4}$ in (1480 mm)
Hardwood for blocks, 4	$2\frac{3}{8}$ x $2\frac{3}{8}$ in (60 x 60 mm)	1 ft (305 mm)
Hardwood for mitered frame, 4	$2\frac{3}{4}$ x $\frac{5}{8}$ in (70 x 16 mm)	6 ft $1\frac{1}{2}$ in (1861 mm)
Hardwood for scotia molding, 3, and infills, 6	$\frac{3}{4}$ x $\frac{5}{8}$ in (19 x 16 mm)	5 ft $\frac{1}{2}$ in (1542 mm)
DRAWERS		
Hardwood for top front, 1	$4\frac{3}{8}$ x $\frac{3}{4}$ in (111 x 19 mm)	1 ft $3\frac{3}{8}$ in (390 mm)
Hardwood for second front, 1	5 x $\frac{3}{4}$ in (125 x 19 mm)	1 ft $3\frac{3}{8}$ in (390 mm)
Hardwood for third, fourth and fifth fronts, 3	6 x $\frac{3}{4}$ in (150 x 19 mm)	3 ft $10\frac{1}{8}$ in (1170 mm)
Hardwood for sixth and seventh fronts, 2	$6\frac{3}{8}$ x $\frac{3}{4}$ in (162 x 19 mm)	2 ft $6\frac{3}{4}$ in (780 mm)
Hardwood for top sides, 2	$4\frac{3}{8}$ x $\frac{3}{8}$ in (111 x 10 mm)	2 ft $4\frac{1}{2}$ in (720 mm)
Hardwood for second sides, 2	5 x $\frac{3}{8}$ in (125 x 10 mm)	2 ft $4\frac{1}{2}$ in (720 mm)
Hardwood for third, fourth and fifth sides, 6	6 x $\frac{3}{8}$ in (150 x 10 mm)	7 ft $1\frac{1}{2}$ in (2160 mm)
Hardwood for sixth and seventh sides, 4	$6\frac{3}{8}$ x $\frac{3}{8}$ in (162 x 10 mm)	4 ft 9 in (1440 mm)
Hardwood for first back, 1	$3\frac{3}{4}$ x $\frac{3}{8}$ in (95 x 10 mm)	1 ft $3\frac{3}{8}$ in (390 mm)
Hardwood for second back, 1	$4\frac{3}{16}$ x $\frac{3}{8}$ in (106 x 10 mm)	1 ft $3\frac{3}{8}$ in (390 mm)
Hardwood for third, fourth and fifth backs, 3	$5\frac{1}{4}$ x $\frac{3}{8}$ in (133 x 10 mm)	3 ft $10\frac{1}{8}$ in (1170 mm)
Hardwood for sixth and seventh backs, 2	$5\frac{3}{4}$ x $\frac{3}{8}$ in (145 x 10 mm)	2 ft $6\frac{3}{8}$ in (780 mm)
Plywood for bottoms, 7	1 ft $2\frac{1}{4}$ in x $\frac{1}{4}$ in (360 x 6 mm)	8 ft 9 in (2660 mm)
Drawer knobs or handles, 14, and woodscrews		

WINE RACK

*This rack, designed to take 24 wine bottles, has been made of cherry with steel rods,
but you can use any decorative hardwood. It is constructed with mortise-and-tenon joints;
for ease and speed, these are best cut on machine tools.*

1 Mark and cut a plywood template for the uprights to 3 ft (915 mm) length; the curve reduces from a width of 2½ in (65 mm) at the widest point to 1¼ in (32 mm) at the ends – a radius of 8 ft 10 in (2690 mm). Mark the four uprights onto the wood, and cut using a table saw and bandsaw.

2 Mark and cut a plywood template for the stretchers to 1 ft 7 in (485 mm) length; the radius is again 8 ft 10 in (2690 mm), and the widest point is 1¼ in (32 mm). Mark and cut the 14 stretchers to length, but do not cut the curves at this stage. Mark and cut the 14 side braces to 9½ in (240 mm).

3 Cut the tenons on the stretchers and side braces. On all stretchers, the 1 in (25 mm) long tenons are centered on the stock, as are the tenons on the top side braces on each side. The lower six pairs of side braces have tenons set against the outward-facing edge, so stretcher and side brace mortises do not impede each other.

4 Cut the stretcher curves using a bandsaw. The top front stretcher and the seven back stretchers have straight back edges, but the lower six front stretchers have curved back edges. Use the plywood template stretcher to mark the curves on the back edges, and cut them as before.

5 Mark mortise positions for the uprights on scrap timber, and transfer onto the uprights. The lower back stretchers are 1¼ in (32 mm) lower than the corresponding front stretchers so that the wine bottles sit horizontally. Both top stretchers sit flush with the top of the uprights.

6 Cut the mortises in the uprights, using a drill press and cleaning up with a sharp chisel. Dry-assemble the uprights, stretchers and side braces, checking for square, and make any adjustments necessary. When satisfied, disassemble the rack.

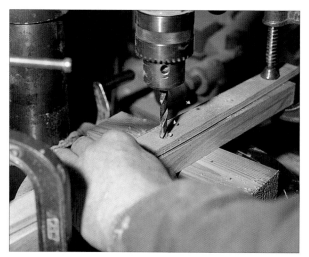

7 Using the stretcher template, mark the ¹/₂ in (12 mm) central holes for the steel rods in the stretchers. The centers of the two outer holes are 4¹/₄ in (110 mm) from the center of the first hole. Drill the holes right through the stretchers, except for the underside of the top stretchers and the top of the bottom stretchers, where the hole is stopped ¹/₂ in (12 mm) into the timber.

8 Finish all the upright and stretcher curves on a sander. Cut the three front steel rods to 2 ft 6 in (760 mm) and the three back steel rods to 2 ft 7¹/₄ in (790 mm), and slot them through the stretchers. Position the stretchers against the uprights.

9 Glue the mortise-and-tenon joints on the front and back assemblies, and gently knock them together before clamping with bar clamps. Leave to dry.

10 Dry-assemble the front and back assemblies and the side braces. The two top side braces sit a little higher than the uprights; mark the curves on them, disassemble and plane the curve onto the top side braces.

11 Glue the side brace joints, insert the side braces and assemble the rack, checking for square, and clamp with bar clamps. Leave to dry, then clean up and finish.

72

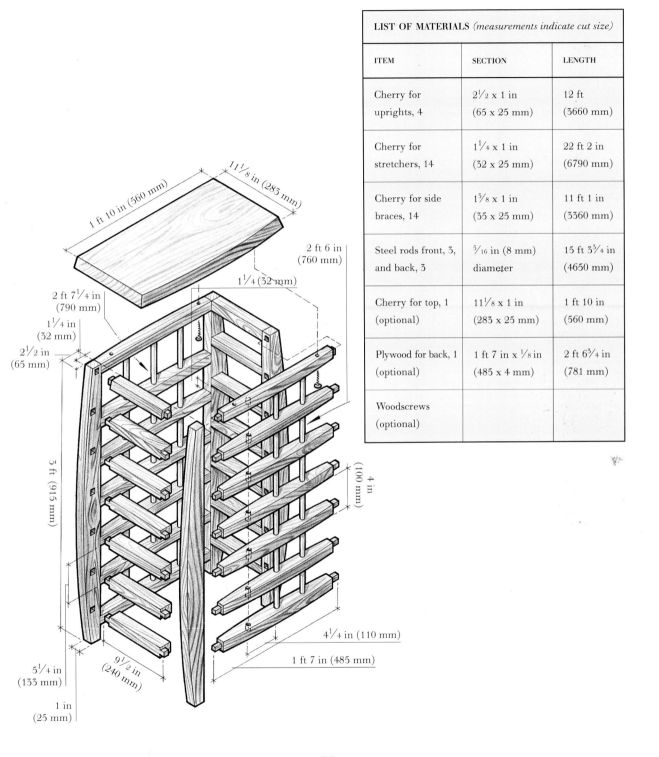

1 ft 10 in (560 mm)

11⅛ in (283 mm)

2 ft 6 in
(760 mm)

1¼ (32 mm)

2 ft 7¼ in
(790 mm)

1¼ in
(32 mm)

2½ in
(65 mm)

3 ft (915 mm)

4 in
(100 mm)

4¼ in (110 mm)

1 ft 7 in (485 mm)

9½ in
(240 mm)

5¼ in
(133 mm)

1 in
(25 mm)

LIST OF MATERIALS *(measurements indicate cut size)*

ITEM	SECTION	LENGTH
Cherry for uprights, 4	2½ x 1 in (65 x 25 mm)	12 ft (3660 mm)
Cherry for stretchers, 14	1¼ x 1 in (32 x 25 mm)	22 ft 2 in (6790 mm)
Cherry for side braces, 14	1⅜ x 1 in (35 x 25 mm)	11 ft 1 in (3360 mm)
Steel rods front, 3, and back, 3	5/16 in (8 mm) diameter	15 ft 3¾ in (4650 mm)
Cherry for top, 1 (optional)	11⅛ x 1 in (283 x 25 mm)	1 ft 10 in (560 mm)
Plywood for back, 1 (optional)	1 ft 7 in x ⅛ in (485 x 4 mm)	2 ft 6¾ in (781 mm)
Woodscrews (optional)		

LIMING AND FRENCH POLISHING

Liming or lightening wood creates a distressed effect which is popular for both traditional and modern pieces. The mirror-like sheen of a French polish can be deceptive – it may appear labor-intensive, but you can achieve stunning effects easily and cheaply.

Polishing brushes
Use a polisher's mop or a lacquer brush to apply French polish. They are both available in a range of styles to suit your needs.

Materials for liming
White liming wax, steel wood and wire brush are the basic liming tools. A phosphor bronze wire brush is ideal, but you can use any clean wire brush.

Liming Wood

Liming, the traditional method for lightening the color of oak, has regained its popularity in the last couple of decades, particularly for kitchens and bathrooms, although there is no reason why it cannot be used to create a striking decorative effect anywhere in the house. This technique is usually applied to oak but it can be used to stain other heavily grained woods.

There are four alternative methods for liming; the old-fashioned technique uses slaked lime, but this needs to be prepared and is unpleasant to use; proprietary liming waxes tend to mark easily, so although they produce a good finish on decorative furniture or panels, they are unsuitable for use in a kitchen or bathroom; a quick limed effect can be achieved by sealing the wood thoroughly and applying and wiping off thinned white undercoat or ordinary household emulsion paint, then sealing the result with varnish; however, the most effective method is to use liming paste,

which is available from a number of manufacturers. The methods of application that are described below are suitable for liming pastes and waxes.

Whatever method you use, it is important to prepare the wood thoroughly before liming, if you are to have any chance of achieving a good finish. The aim is to remove the soft tissues from the deep pores in open-grained wood, so that they can be filled with the liming paste. You can follow these steps for preparation on both new and old wood; they are particularly useful for wood that is being refinished, because even proprietary strippers tend to leave small amounts of the old finish in the pores.

Preparing the Wood

After sanding the wood smooth, remove any residual grease with mineral spirits. Next, wet the surface of the wood with fresh water and allow this to soften the tissues. Using a clean wire brush, scrub the wood in the direction of the grain – this will scrape out the soft fibers of the timber and open the pores. Check your progress at regular intervals, to make sure that the open pores look even over the whole surface. When dry, lightly sand the surface to remove any roughness, and dust down with a hard brush to remove any last traces of sawdust.

If you intend to stain the wood before liming, to produce a darker, more contrasted finish, or a colored finish (see p. 76), apply the stain or dye at this stage and seal it with a coat of transparent shellac, then let this dry.

Using Liming Paste

Even if you are only liming a small surface or object, bear in mind that the paste or wax can get everywhere, and that it is very difficult to wash out completely, so wear old clothes when liming any woodwork.

Dip a clean cloth into the liming paste, and rub it well into the grain, using circular strokes to bed it in. Liming pastes dry very hard, so do not apply them too thickly – you may find that thinning them with a little water produces a paste that is easier to use – and rub in only as much as is needed. Leave to dry completely, and remove any cloth marks by lightly sanding. Wipe off the dust, and apply a surface coating.

Water-based liming pastes will accept just about any surface finish, from wax polish to sanding sealer, French polish, and even varnishes and lacquers; obviously, the harder-wearing finishes are the most suitable for the everyday wear and tear in the kitchen. As with all finishes, take time to follow the manufacturer's instructions fully, otherwise all your hard work could be wasted, and you may have to start again.

Using Liming Wax

For liming waxes, prepare the wood as described above, and apply the coat of wax as for liming paste. Then use a clean cloth to wipe across the grain of the wood while still leaving the wax in the open pores of the wood. Leave for about 10–15 minutes, then use another clean cloth to burnish along the direction of the grain. Leave overnight before applying clear wax polish.

Scraping out the fibers
Once the wood has been softened by water, scrub the wood in the direction of the grain to remove the soft fibers and open the pores.

Applying paste or wax
You can use either a cloth or fine steel wool to apply liming paste or wax. Rub well into the grain, using circular strokes.

Cleaning the wax
Use a clean cloth or clean steel wool to clean surplus wax off the surface of the wood before applying clear wax or varnish.

Applying the polish
Never overbrush French polish – apply it with long strokes of the brush from end to end on flat surfaces.

Corners and round sections
Always ensure that the brush or mop is not overloaded with polish, otherwise you will have problems with drips.

Buffing the shine
The deep glow of a French-polished and waxed piece of furniture repays the practice and work you put into it.

Colored Limed Finishes

Pastel blue and green limed finishes have become popular for kitchen furniture, and there is no reason why you can't experiment with your own shades to create eye-catching limed colors. To achieve this effect, one technique is to stain the wood the required color first and then apply the paste to draw out some of the color. Alternatively, to achieve a more uniform color, add a little amount of bright-colored water-based dye to the paste and mix it in well. Once diluted in the paste, the strong color is replaced by a subtle pastel shade. The method of application is exactly the same as for plain white liming paste, and you can use the same surface finishes.

Simple French Polishing

For many woodworkers, French polishing is a daunting and difficult method of finishing, steeped in mystique and requiring almost limitless patience and skill. In fact, although creating the mirror-like glossy finish found on concert pianos and Victorian pieces does take practice and a high degree of concentration, using French polish to make a beautiful finish is one of the easiest, cheapest, and most versatile methods of all.

You do not need much equipment to get started. A polisher's mop or lacquer brush is the most expensive piece, but will last for a long time if treated well. Mops are round in section and are available in a range of sizes determined by a number – the greater the number, the larger the mop; a No. 8 is a versatile starting point. Flat-section lacquer brushes fit well into long internal corners, and are also available in a number of sizes measured in inches or millimeters like a household paintbrush: a 1½ in (38 mm) brush will do most work. Lacquer brushes are also useful for applying stains and oils. Finally you will need button, garnet, or white French polish (the difference is in the color – button is mid-brown, garnet is dark red-brown, and white is used on pale woods), denatured alcohol, a jar, and 240-grit sandpaper or finer. The best way to practice is on samples; these need to be about 3 ft (610 mm) square or a similar rectangular size. You can use veneered manufactured boarding, which needs minimal preparation, or prepare pieces from solid wood and run a molding around the edge to gain more experience. Pine is not really a suitable timber. You can stain the pieces if you wish, but be aware that if you use spirit-based stain, you may encounter the problem of the polish pulling off the stain.

Applying French polish is a totally different technique from painting. There are two basic rules: do not overload the mop or brush, and do not overbrush. Apply the polish in long strokes from end to end, always dropping the brush just inside the leading edge, otherwise you will have polish running over the ends. Always work off ends. If you do have a run over, wipe it away immediately with your finger. The edges that run parallel to the brushstrokes are also susceptible to running over, as are surface edges; run a finger along them to wipe off any excess, and along the underneath surfaces that you cannot see.

Slightly overlap each stroke onto the previous one; if you miss a small area, leave it – the second coat will deal with the problem. Speed and confidence are the secrets of applying a first coat over spirit stain; when working on bare wood, you can brush out the polish a little more. Another tip is not to have the polish too thick on the mop or brush. Polishes vary according to the manufacturer, and consistency is a matter of judgement. If overlapping is a problem, try thinning the polish with 10–20 per cent denatured alcohol. Allow to dry – in a reasonably warm environment, this should not take very long.

Building the Layers

Check the surface with your fingertips to see if it is still smooth. If it is, apply a second coat straight away. If it feels slightly rough, lightly paper over it along the grain, using very fine sand or glasspaper; be especially careful with edges and end corners, because it is easy to take off the polish. Look hard for hairs that may have come off the mop or brush, or other debris, allow to harden, and paper them out before the next coat. If you spot bristles when applying polish, do not stop to remove them, but continue as above.

Sanding produces very fine white dust which must be removed before applying subsequent coats. Tack cloths are often used to remove this dust, but a better method is to sweep the palm of your clean hand from one end of the work to the other – the natural oil in your skin will pick up the dust. Wipe your hand on your apron and repeat to cover the entire surface. If you use 0000-grade steel wool as an abrasive between coats, be extra careful to remove all the bits from the working area; if even a few are picked up by a mop or brush, they can be spread over the whole surface and make more work for you.

On one of the samples, leave the second coat to harden for a few hours, then apply some wax polish with 0000-grade steel wool and buff it up. This produces a fairly low luster that is perfectly smooth. If you want to achieve a higher degree of sheen, you can apply further coats of wax polish and buff them.

On the other samples, repeat with as many applications of French polish as you like, leaving each coat to harden and fill the grain a little more, and then sand. If you apply many coats, you will reach a stage where the polish is too soft to continue; leave it for several hours to harden before resuming. Use a polishing pad to finish off the most important areas which are free of internal corners. By practicing on samples in this way, you will soon gain confidence and the knowledge of how finishes work on different woods, and how many coats to apply.

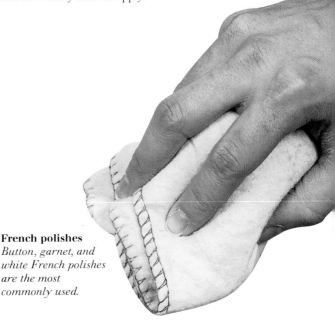

French polishes
Button, garnet, and white French polishes are the most commonly used.

INDEX

ACKNOWLEDGMENTS

Makers

George Buchanan: Spice Cabinet (p. 36); Wheelback Kitchen Chair (p. 30).
Peter Bishop: Plate Display Unit (p. 20); Shaker Drawers (p. 64);
(Original design by Mark Finney).
Frank Delicata: Plate Drying Rack (p. 10).
Mike Denley: Cherry Dining Table (p. 14); Kitchen Wall Unit (p. 46).
Lester Haines: Wine Rack (p. 70).
John Harding: Limed Cupboard (p.24); (steps by Peter Bishop);
Oak Breakfront (p. 52); (steps by Bob Piper).
Bob Piper (Channel Rye Ltd): Country Kitchen Table (p. 40);
French Windows (p.58).

Thanks also to Helen Adkins, Eric Kendall and Janet Swarbrick
for their valued contribution.

Suppliers

Garden trug and terracotta pots (cover, p. 40) and plants (p. 58) courtesy of
The Chelsea Gardener, London.
Rug and chairs (p. 14), table and chairs (p. 58) courtesy of
The Pier, London.

Stylists

Claire Worthington: pp. 20, 46, 64, 70.
Alison Verity: pp. 14, 40, 58.

Photographers

Geoff Dann: pp. 14-15, 40–41, 58–59, 64, 70.
Sampson Lloyd: pp. 53, 54, 56.